The DRUG ADDICT
as a PATIENT

The DRUG ADDICT
as a PATITENT

By MARIE NYSWANDER, M.D.
Senior Supervising Psychiatrist,
Post Graduate Center for Psychotherapy;
Consultant, New York City Department of Health;
President, National Advisory Council on Narcotics

Grune & Stratton
New York and London

First printing, June 1956
Second printing, December 1971

GRUNE & STRATTON, INC.
111 Fifth Avenue, New York, New York 10003

Library of Congress Catalog Card Number   55-12227
International Standard Book Number   0-8089-0351-9

Printed in the United States of America

CONTENTS

PREFACE

FORTY YEARS have elapsed since the Harrison Narcotic Act went into effect. Today, estimates of the number of drug addicts in the United States range all the way from a conservative 60,000 to an outside figure of 1,000,000. During the past six years, institutions have noted an alarming increase in addiction among adolescents and young adults—in some instances up to 200 per cent over the previous decade's figures.

Only a slight impact has been made on drug addiction by various groups and individuals who have had the foresight to recognize the serious menace of the problem. Public Health officials, social workers, probation officers, as well as private civic and religious groups working with youths, are struggling heroically but, unfortunately, in large part unsuccessfully, to ameliorate the devastation of addiction.

One of the reasons for the poverty of results is that many drug addicts have "gone underground" since the Harrison Act was passed. This has influenced adversely the data, both qualitatively and quantitatively, that are available for study. As a result we are wont to minimize the importance of addiction as a public health problem. Before joining the staff of the United States Public Health Service Hospital in Lexington, Kentucky, I shared this point of view. I had never seen a drug addict patient, and during my stay there I frequently felt that it would have been a pleasure to miss this experience. "Sick call" was an ordeal for physicians, for we spent several hours a day trying to determine whether each patient was really ill or just trying to obtain drugs by feigning illness. Nights were interrupted by calls to attend patients with alleged gall bladder crises, heart attacks, and every manner of medical emergency, all of which required careful diagnosis on the off-chance that a serious illness might be present.

My fear as I proceeded to break up a group of threatening, enraged women patients would be followed by a conviction that it was useless for the Government to spend large sums of money to shelter and treat them. Efforts to make patients more comfortable in the hospital-prison invariably resulted in flagrant violation—and subsequent revoking—of their new privileges. The medical charts of most patients were thick volumes covering years of compulsory hospitalization and relapses. It seemed to me that there was not one hopeful case.

When I completed my training and had obtained my speciality Boards in Psychiatry and Neurology, I found myself handling the drug addict in the traditionally prescribed manner; namely, immediate prolonged hospitalization and complete withdrawal from the drug. But as time went on, practical considerations necessitated a deviation in some cases from the accepted mode of handling. In sharing my experiences with my medical colleagues I discovered that they, too, had been treating their patients as individuals with human problems, utilizing varied family and community resources, instead of arbitrarily sending them to institutions. As time went by, my outlook underwent a change, due largely to successful results that were being obtained by what I had considered to be an unorthodox approach. I learned that my experience at Lexington had to be supplemented; I came to realize that any form of compulsory treatment had considerable limitation.

This book, drawn from my own experiences, and those of other physicians who have handled addiction, sets forth various methods of approach used in private practice, and is an attempt to bring a large-scale subject within the scope of a handbook. While it is geared to physicians in general practice, it is hoped that it will be useful to a wide variety of professional people who are thrown into contact with addicts—social workers, civic planners, hospital administrators and probation officers.

I have also included material on the new horizons in the treatment of drug addiction that are beginning to appear. Thus, in August, 1955, The New York Academy of Medicine published the report of a group of physicians appointed in the spring of the same year to make a thorough study of drug addiction. The Committee's recommendations, of great practical and historical importance, have been included, with their permission, as a separate section in this volume (Chapter X).

The book describes a recently advocated approach that endorses the management and treatment of the drug addict by the family physician. Also included are the successful methods used in treating addicts in Great Britain, methods which are currently arousing great interest in this country.

I wish to acknowledge my indebtedness to my husband, Leonard Wallace Robinson, and Dr. Lewis R. Wolberg and Duncan Mackintosh, for their encouragement and helpful suggestions; and to Elma T. Wadsworth for valuable editorial assistance in preparing this manuscript for publication. When several attempts to obtain certain necessary information from Great Britain had failed, Dr. Jeffrey Bishop offered to do the necessary research. He also obtained permission to include material from many articles copyrighted by the Controller of Her Britannic Majesty's Stationery Office.

Mention should be made of the help given me by Dr. A. Wikler and other workers in the field of drug addiction, whose personal communications and publications yielded a great deal of useful information.

Lastly, thanks are due to my own patients and the addicted patients of other physicians. For it is their courage and struggle, against great odds, which make our efforts to help them well worth while.

MARIE NYSWANDER, MD.

New York, N. Y.
January 1956

To My Mother
Dorothy Bird Nyswander

I. Drug Addiction in the United States: Past and Present

DRUG ADDICTION is a distinct medical entity which ravages the patient, destroys the entire fabric of his life, and adversely affects the lives of his family and others close to him.

As in every major disease, the patient is helpless before its destructive inroads. Struggle as he may, the curious and inexorable process overwhelms him. No outer moral compulsion can stay it; no authoritarian decree can cut it short. Punishment is meaningless, imprisonment futile, in halting the relentless course of the disease.

Who has been appointed to treat this pandemic scourge? In the United States, due to an unfortunate series of historical events, the criminal underworld has taken over the task of treating the addict; only from this underworld can he obtain relief for his terrifying symptoms. Prevented by law from administering to the addict, physicians in the United States have had to stand by helplessly as this tragedy has unfolded.

How has this situation developed? What chain of circumstances has separated the physician from a problem authorities have come to believe should be placed in his hands? To find the answers to these questions we must go back to the mid-nineteenth century.

Before the addictive power of opium and other drugs was recognized, at least a million people in this country were exposed to addiction through patent medicines and physicians' prescriptions. Because of the soothing and analgesic properties of opium and its derivatives, these drugs were used indiscriminately to relieve everything from simple headache to angina pectoris. Various remedies with a narcotic content of 5 to 10 per cent were sold without restraint over the counters of pharmacies all over the country. Through such wonder-working medicaments as Mrs. Winslow's Soothing Syrup, Dr. Cole's Catarrh Cure and Perkins' Diarrhea Mixture, incredible amounts of opium, morphine, codeine and cocaine were spooned into children as well as adults. Every well-equipped home had a rosewood chest, counterpart of the present day medicine cabinet, with its ball of opium and its bottle of paregoric. Our hardy ancestors were indeed well buffered against the manifold pains to which human flesh is heir.

Under these conditions, with the physician ignorant of the evil effects of narcotics, addiction spread with the speed and thoroughness of an influenza epidemic. By 1863, twenty years after Alexander Wood had invented the hypodermic needle, estimates of addiction in the United States ran as high as 4 per cent of the population.[1]

It was not until the eighteen nineties that the medical profession began to recognize the danger lurking in these drugs and to launch plans to bring some order out of the chaos. Articles and books exposing the horrors of addiction poured from the nation's presses. Local medical societies appointed committees to study drug addiction. By publicizing the results and educating the general physician in the proper use of narcotics they hoped to be able to cope with this problem. By 1900, institutions for treating drug addiction dotted the country from coast to coast. Newspapers and journals carried advertisements of cures for drug addiction. Dr. Samuel Collins, whose product *Antidote* was the most popular one, admitted that he had spent $300,000 in advertising alone!

Further confusion followed heroin's discovery in 1898. Since it relieved morphine withdrawal symptoms, it was at first believed to be a cure for morphine addiction and was rapidly substituted for the latter drug in cough medicines and tonics. Years after its use became widespread, medical journals carried articles stressing its non-addicting properties. Why fully twelve years passed before the medical profession became sufficiently aroused to proclaim its pernicious effects is still a mystery.

One of the great pioneers in the early vigorous movement to combat drug addiction was Dr. Charles Towns of New York City. He was the first to recognize the tripartite syndrome which we call drug addiction and to break it down into its component parts. The manifestations he clearly described still hold good today: (1) the compulsive need; (2) the inevitable increase in tolerance and hence in drug intake; (3) the characteristic relapse after withdrawal. It was Dr. Towns who first proposed a strict and systematic control of narcotics by physicians, and in fact he drafted one of the earliest laws designed to bring the situation under control. Known as the Boylan Law, it was passed by the New York Legislature in 1904.

At this point came a decisive and, as it turned out, tragic occurrence. Although Dr. Towns' proposal included carefully detailed provisions for the treatment of the addict population, this part was dropped before the Boylan Law was finally passed. The Harrison Narcotic Act, which became a law in 1914, was modeled on the Boylan Law. And it, too, omitted the vital measures concerned with the physician's role in treating the disease.

Omission of this provision was, within a decade, to have disastrous results. Both the Boylan Law and the Harrison Narcotic Act were designed to control the production, manufacture and distribution of addictive drugs by making it necessary to register all transactions, however insignificant. In addition, it was specified that only physicians could prescribe these drugs.

This proviso, which outlawed over-the-counter traffic in drugs and sent all addicts to the physicians for treatment, was applauded on all sides, but not for long. As their supplies were exhausted, thousands of addicts formed queues at physicians' offices. Physicians were swamped and physically unable to treat the addicts as patients. Their offices became, in effect, dispensaries.

Many addicts voluntarily entered hospitals in an effort to break their habit. Doors were wide open, for neither physicians nor hospitals had the strong prejudice against this group which later developed. However, within a year or two of the time the original Harrison Narcotic Act went into effect, physicians had seen countless addicts and, through trial and error, study and pooling of knowledge, they were well on the way to becoming experts in diagnosing and treating this disease. They learned that relapse is an inevitable factor to be reckoned with in the addiction syndrome and that the success of withdrawal treatment depends on a flexible method, readily adaptable to the individual patient. They began to recognize certain psychological and neurological components of the disease—and to fore-see that a tremendous research program would be necessary before the problem could be mastered completely.

It is important at this juncture to realize that the drug addict before 1914 had little or no involvement with criminal activity. He carried on his job, maintained his home and family life. His illness did not inflict injury on any one other than himself. He considered himself and was considered by others to be grappling with a definite and difficult problem and he expected to obtain treatment in a legitimate manner.

It rapidly became apparent that the Harrison Narcotic Act would have to be improved and strengthened to make for better control. Here a sinister angle was introduced. Treatment for the addict had been ignored in the original act; amendments and certain court decisions compounded the error, so that the addict was gradually forced out of the role of the legitimately ill into the role of the willful criminal. The United States Supreme Court's interpretation of certain new legislation made it more and more precarious for the physician to treat addiction.

This incongruous situation developed by stages. The Harrison Narcotic Act was basically a revenue code, and enforcement was placed in the hands of the Bureau of Internal Revenue. Federal agents were of necessity empowered to investigate and prosecute violations. There is no gainsaying the fact that there were numerous loopholes in the original Act—loopholes that had to be plugged to insure enforcement. But, upheld by Supreme Court decisions, the Bureau extended its activities until it assumed control of the domestic narcotic traffic and of medical treatment of addiction as well.

Severe enforcement procedures were put into effect. Many physicians were imprisoned for administering to their patients, and overnight a million victims of a horrifying illness were transformed into criminals. When the legislators and enforcement officers ignored the terrible needs imposed on the addict by his disease, his one alternative was to turn to the underworld for relief. Dr. Towns raised his voice in alarm:

"Why has the deplorable general condition arisen? The general medical practitioner does not know which way to turn to meet the unfavorable conditions that have grown out of the lack of proper provision for the definite medical treatment of this type of patient. . . . Worthy persons addicted to narcotics found they were unable to get them through legitimate channels and thus have been forced to get them through other channels."[2]

Dr. Howe[11] has summarized it, "thus, virulent criminality was added to what was formerly simple immorality."

Month by month the addict met a stiffer attitude on all sides. At length the Federal Nacrotics Control Board came up with their solution: compulsory treatment, and the Board's successor since 1930, the present Bureau of Narcotics in the Treasury Department, still considers compulsory treatment the only road to complete cure. Article 117 of Regulation 35, 1919, states that "All cases of chronic opiate intoxication except those with an incurable malady and the infirm can be treated successfully." It was naïvely assumed that the drug addict would prefer compulsory withdrawal treatment to paying the prohibitive prices demanded in the newly-flourishing illicit drug market. Or perhaps it was believed that he would be unable to meet these prices and would thus be driven to treatment by his severe withdrawal symptoms.

Ignorance of the true nature of the drug addict's malady had further ramifications, for the Bureau's entire program carried the implication that relapse to drugs is a crime. Not the treatment but the patient himself was assumed to be at fault, and he was dealt with accordingly. The logic, to say nothing of the humanity, of such an attitude is open to question.

Many outstanding physicians of the time evaluated the situation accurately. Dr. Charles Terry in 1920 said:

> "If the Harrison Narcotic Act and its regulations and administrative policies are based on the assumption that addiction is little more than the expression of a vicious criminal habit or desire . . . then they are right to counter with exclusive handling. . . . If, on the other hand, addiction consists of a pathological entity beyond the individual's power to control . . . how can they be expected to control it?"[3]

By this time, U.S. medical practitioners were thoroughly intimidated. Prosecution of a number of physicians had made others doubly wary. Of the 8,100 physicians practicing in New York City, less than forty continued to prescribe narcotics for addicts. And the Bureau seized upon this fact further to discredit the physician's role. These physicians, besieged by addicts, were of necessity giving out a large number of prescriptions. Accused of "trafficking in drugs," they were all indicted. The term "trafficking physician" carried such opprobrium that practitioners who valued their reputation could not afford to administer drugs no matter how ill the addict. The Bureau had won the day in New York, and the private physician's right to treat the ill had been abrogated.

To combat the public health problems created by the pandemic spread of drug addiction and its new handmaiden—crime—city health departments throughout the nation set up dispensaries and clinics for the medical treatment of drug addiction. From 1920 to 1924, about forty cities tried this method and many of the experiments were extremely rewarding. The clinics were making distinct headway in dissolving the alliance between underworld and addict, collecting valuable data, gaining new insight into the personal and sociological problems of the addict.

The Bureau of Internal Revenue then selected the New York City clinic, the weakest and least representative of the lot, for investigation. They exposed its operation strictly from the legal viewpoint and widely publicized its failure. There is no doubt that it was a failure, but the other clinics, which the public was not informed about, were anything but failures. However, they were soon to be closed on the strength of the one example. An examination of the much-quoted failure of the New York clinic reveals the following highlights. It was opened on April 10, 1919, and lasted only nine months. It was ill-planned and ill-run from the outset. Few if any specialists in drug addiction were consulted, and the actual set-up for dispensing the drugs was badly handled. Drugs were to be administered only to those addicts who wished to withdraw themselves. No provisions were made for the symptom known as relapse; no cognizance was taken of the complicated psychological and physiological problems that go hand-in-hand with addiction.

The Director, Dr. S. Dana Hubbard, in his final report summed up the Clinic's approach to drug addiction as follows:

"Our opinion is that this habit is not a mysterious disease. . . . It is simply a degrading, debasing habit. . . . It can be safely said without contradiction that drug addiction, per se, is not a disease any more than excessive indulgence in cigarettes."[10]

When the clinic opened, 7464 patients appeared. Queues stretched around city blocks and confusion reigned. Each individual was given a twenty-four-hour supply of narcotics and told to report each day for a decreased dosage. The clinic administrators' lack of knowledge is clearly shown by the initial dosage decided upon. Experienced physicians at the time knew that $1/4$ grain of morphine q.i.d. was sufficient to prevent severe withdrawal symptoms in most addicts, yet the New York clinic handed out 15 grains to each addict regardless of the size of his habit. The natural consequence was that many upped their habit immediately, making it more and more difficult to maintain, in view of the daily reduction plan.

No attempt was made either to register the applicants or to examine them physically to ascertain whether they were, in fact, true addicts. They could, and did, move from line to line and got several doses if they wished—a fact triumphantly reported by Treasury Agents who were on the spot posing as addicts.

These rational explanations for the clinic's failure were never mentioned. The exposé was for the sole purpose of showing that illicit traffic continued and even thrived throughout the short life of the clinic, for of course the addict supplemented his daily decreasing dosage to keep in drug-balance. Even so, there were positive aspects which could have been stressed about the functioning of this poorly run experiment. For instance, an astonishing number of addicts, by appearing at the clinic, clearly manifested their distaste for the underworld network that had enmeshed them. Two thousand of these addicts availed themselves of the clinic's offer to provide hospitalization for withdrawal. Any project of such magnitude and complexity is faced with a few years of adjustment, a time for ironing out the kinks, but the New York clinic was actually defeated by its own absurd organization. With much fanfare it was closed on January 15, 1920.

Great Britain attacked the problem from another angle entirely. The Ministry of Health was at the time launching its new Dangerous Drug Act—similar in content to the Harrison Act, but how differently enforced. Education and encouragement, instead of indictment and prosecution, were the order of the day.[4] Sound basic tenets laid down for the physician prepared him for his task. With help and encouragement, he was told, many people could be successfully withdrawn from drugs. He would encounter others who could not be successfully withdrawn but might have to be maintained on drugs throughout their lives. Relapse was an inevitable part of the illness. Eventual success would depend on his maintaining contact with the patient both on and off drugs. Given this orientation, he was left to make his own decisions. Sensitive to the physical and mental distress of the patient, the physician kept him stabilized on drugs until such time as both agreed that withdrawal treatment could be instituted. Great Britain within six years made considerable progress under the Dangerous Drug Act, while the United States was pursuing the course we have outlined.

The Bureau maintained a discreet silence on the clinics operating outside of New York. Brief though their existence turned out to be, it is now clear that they constituted the only constructive, country-wide medical experiment for coping with drug addiction to date. Of the forty in operation at that time, the most outstanding were: New Orleans, under the direction of Dr. Swords (opened in 1919 and closed in 1921); Shreveport, under the direction of Dr. Butler (opened in 1921 and closed in 1924); and Los Angeles, under the direction of Dr. Bucher (opened in 1920 and closed in 1921). The reason given for the closing of the Los Angeles clinic was that "it was the only one left in the U.S.," according to the agent charged with this task.

The success of the Shreveport and New Orleans clinics was due to the combined efforts of courageous physicians and progressive-minded local authorities. Addicts everywhere are in a continuous emergency situation.[9] New Orleans, a main port, had its share of smuggling activity, and in both cities the poor economic circumstances of many addicts had made a community medical program imperative. The clinics took full advantage of existing expert knowledge and clearly stated their objectives:

1. To relieve the addict's suffering. It was freely acknowledged that too little was actually known about the entire complex problem to expect permanent cures.

2. To offset illegal trafficking in drugs—the addict's only source—by legally supplying him with such drugs.

3. To keep addiction from spreading further.

4. To reduce the incidence of thievery and other criminal activity resulting from the addict's need to maintain his drug balance.

The New Orleans clinic tried to protect its addicts in every possible way. They were not registered and the local police cooperated by non-interference. The clinic directors felt that any police activity might send addicts scurrying back to the underworld. The police, primed by the clinic staff, bent over backward to accord addicts the understanding and sympathetic help due any sick person

In its two years, the New Orleans clinic more than justified the faith and hard work of its staff. It had given temporary relief to addicts at a minimum cost. It had helped the unemployable drifters in this group to return to employment and resume family life. Since no new recruits came through the dispensary during its existence, "contagion" in this community had ostensibly been broken up. As shown by police records, it had reduced petty thievery and other criminal activity. In addition, it had managed to operate on the slim margin of profit between the wholesale price of morphine and the low retail price paid by the addict.

New Orleans' experience was repeated with variations in Shreveport, Louisiana. State and city authorities as well as religious leaders gave their unqualified support to the clinic. Shreveport's success was particularly significant inasmuch as a previous clinic based on compulsory treatment had failed.

The Los Angeles Clinic's director, Dr. Bucher, started out by adhering strictly to the forcible reduction method laid down by law. But he soon found that after reaching a certain point the addicts invariably sought more drugs from underworld peddlers to supplement their decreased dosage. When he relaxed these stringent rules, the patients' response was dramatic: they began to leave the relief rolls, stay within the law and find jobs to sustain themselves and their families.

Of this aspect Dr. Bucher said:

"It must be accepted that unless drug-balance is maintained addicts return to illicit supplies. . . . It would seem fair to accept the fact that a worker and a producer is of more value to the community than a non-worker and a dependent or perchance a criminal, even though he is suffering from an involuntary chronic disease or a self-inflicted one."[8]

When this clinic was summarily closed by the Bureau of Internal Revenue, community leaders protested, but to no avail. Dr. L. M. Powers, City Health Commissioner, expressed the views of many when he said, "There has been some unseen motive prompting much opposition to clinics, which I have not yet been able to comprehend."

And so it went. One by one the forty clinics were closed by order of the Commissioner of Internal Revenue, and with their closing went the addict's last hope of proper treatment. Through its interpretation and administration of a revenue measure, the Federal government indirectly gained control of medical treatment of addiction and thus endangered the physician's time-honored relationship with his patient.

The present punitive approach to the problem of drug addiction seems to have been no deterrent to the addict, motivated by his craving for drugs, nor to the non-addict dealer, motivated solely by huge profits. Neither has illicit drug traffic been suppressed nor have our laws succeeded in preventing the spread of addiction. On the contrary, there appears to be a higher percentage of addicts among youths and young adults now than before the Harrison Act went into effect.

Even in the face of present hard-won knowledge of the addiction syndrome, the Bureau of Narcotics consistently holds that compulsory hopitalization is the only solution.[8] The many psychological and social components are ignored, and therein lies the trouble. It is unfortunately these very factors which have been found to be the crux of any successful and lasting treatment of addicts.

The heads of the Bureau of Narcotics have met any and all criticism by restating and reaffirming the legality of their position. The Supreme Court has twice declared the Harrison Act constitutional solely as a revenue measure and as an exercise in the Federal power to tax. Whether these decisions have automatically conferred on the Treasury Department the sole power to administer to the sick addict is something which has come to be widely challenged. Certain legal minds believe that one of the pivotal cases (U.S. vs. Behrman, in 1922), which the Treasury Department cites as authority for its interpretation of the law, has been repudiated by a later Supreme Court decision (U.S. vs. Linder, in 1924).[5]

Incidentally, following the Behrman case, the Bureau of Narcotics declared it had become necessary "to investigate and to resort to legal procedures to penalize that physician who willfully prescribes or directly sells narcotic drugs merely for the gratification and perpetuation of narcotic drug addiction." The term *gratification,* which crept in at this point, implies willful indulgence in a vicious habit which one could control if he wished; experienced workers in the field have found this to be far from the truth in the case of narcotic addiction. Judge Cornelia P. Collins in 1922 said of the Federal court's interpretation of the Harrison Act, in relation to its limitation of the physician's treatment of the addict:

"It seems to me that the commissioners have exceeded any authority conferred on them by law, have superseded the rights of the State and have even gone beyond the expressed provisions of the Harrison Narcotic Act."[3]

Dr. L. C. Scott, then acting assistant surgeon of the U. S. Public Health Service, in 1923 made a plea for more humane treatment of the addict and correctly predicted that criminality would continue to increase unless the physician regained control of the illness.[6, 7]

Under the law, physicians are allowed to prescribe narcotics to patients for the relief of pain associated with disease; and to addicts in the course of withdrawal treatment in a definite manner laid down by Federal regulations. They may not prescribe drugs to keep an addict comfortable if he refuses withdrawal even though he might thereby be able to lead a useful work and family life, stay on the right side of the law, and in time be ready to undergo withdrawal.

The situation in this country has been alarming from the time drugs were introduced in the early nineteenth century up to the present. Despite the most stringent restrictive measures ever used in any country to control drug traffic, in forty years drug addiction still is rolling up new recruits, many of them very young with a lifetime of law-dodging ahead, and few authorities think that the epidemic proportions have been appreciably reduced. As with illegal alcoholic consumption during prohibition, there is a scarcity of hard facts and figures. Addicts are not likely to stand up and be counted, and methods of finding out the extent of addiction are extremely unreliable. For example, in 1890 a conservative estimate was 400,000 addicts, or 1 per cent of the population. The maximum estimate was 1,500,000 or nearly 4 per cent. The Bureau of Narcotics, understandably reluctant to give out figures, has admitted that there are probably 60,000 addicts in the United States, roughly of 1 per cent. Other authorities think that 1,000,000 addicts might be closer to the actual number. Certainly there has been one big change—in the addict himself. Once a respectable member of the community, he has become a common criminal. One cannot help drawing a parallel with venereal disease control. For years we turned our backs on the victims of this dread disease and left them to quacks and charlatans. Then came a campaign to change the country's social attitudes through education. Can we not apply the same measures to bring addicts out of hiding, so that they can openly seek help for their disease? Only when addicts are given intelligent and understanding help in place of the widespread public rejection they face today will we be on the road to conquering this problem.

REFERENCES

1. Collins, Samuel: A Treatise on the Habitual Use of Narcotic Poison. LaPorte, Ind., Theriaki, 1887.
2. Towns, Charles: Federal Responsibility in the Solution of the Habit-forming Drug Problem. New York, the author, 1916.
3. Terry, C., and Pellens, M.: The Opium Problem. New York, Commission on Drug Addiction, Bureau of Social Hygiene, 1928.
4. Department Commission on Morphine and Heroin Addiction. London, His Majesty's Stationery Office, 1926.
5. King, Rufus: U. S. vs. Behrman—When the Supreme Court was narcotized. Yale Law J. 62: 736, 1953.
6. Scott, L. C.: Case of the drug addict. Quart. Bull. Louisiana State Board of Health 14: No. 1 (Mar.), 1923.
7. Knopf, S. A.: The one million drug addicts in the United States. M. J. & Rec. 119: 135-139, 1924.
8. Anslinger, H. J.: The physician and the Federal Narcotic Law. Am. J. Psychiat. 102: 609-618, 1946.
9. Terry, C. E.: Symposium on narcotic drug addiction. Recent Experiments in Narcotic Control. American Public Health Association Report, 1920.
10. Hubbard, S. Dana: Some Fallacies Regarding Narcotic Drug Addiction. Department of Health, New York City, Report Series No. 88, 1920.
11. Howe, Hubert S.: A physician's blueprint for the management and prevention of narcotic addiction. New York State J. Med. 55: 341-349, 1955.

II. Pharmacology

THE CENTRAL NERVOUS SYSTEM actually bears the brunt of the chemical action of narcotics. The specific neurophysiologic effects, with a brief résumé of current research on this aspect of drug addiction, are treated separately in the next chapter, *Physiology*. We shall here deal with the drugs which come under the Harrison Narcotic Act, and other drugs considered dangerous because they are either physiologically or psychologically addicting. It is important to bear in mind that addicts also use non-opiate drugs such as Benzedrine and the barbiturates. Cocaine and marijuana, although technically not addicting, are so widely used that a full-scale treatment of narcotics would be incomplete without including them. The chemical families to which these various drugs belong, their uses and abuses will be covered. The last ten years have seen the development of many synthetic morphine equivalent drugs. Interestingly enough, they are found to be clinically interchangeable with the opiates in all major respects, although not chemically related to them.

OPIUM

General Considerations

The use of opium dates back to the pre-Christian era, an early reference being found in the writing of Theophrastus (372-287 B.C.), who called it meconin. Throughout the centuries it has been used as a pain-killer and a sedative. Long before the hypodermic needle was invented, opium was taken orally in the form of a water solution and, in India and China, by smoking.

All opium imported by the United States is in a raw crude form. The principal countries producing this drug commercially are India, Iran, Turkey, China and Yugoslavia. The

14

legitimate trade in crude opium is carried on under strict Federal supervision. Licensed pharmaceutical houses prepare it into morphine and other opiate derivatives.

Opium comes from a specific plant of the poppy family known as *Papaver somniferum*. The collected seeds of this poppy are opened while unripe, yielding a gummy substance which hardens into a black mass. This crude opium is then ready for commercial use. The percentages of opium and of alkaloids in poppy plants varies with individual plants as well as with the country of origin. Thus, Turkish opium has a high amount of morphine, while Iranian opium has a high amount of codeine.

Drug addicts take crude opium either orally or by smoking. The preparation of smoking opium is a secret jealously guarded by Chinese opium specialists. Essentially, this process consists of boiling and filtering the crude opium until the concentrate assumes the form of a gummy mass. Packaged in small boxes or jars known as "toys" or "funs," it is sold to addicts on the black market.

Active Ingredients of Opium

In 1803 the French chemist, Derosne, precipitated a solution of opium and water with potassium carbonate and obtained crystals which he called "salt of opium." Two years later Serturner, a pharmacist of Einbeck in Hanover, obtained the same substance in a pure form, which he called morphine acid meconate.[1] He observed and stressed its properties of neutralizing acids and forming salts. In spite of Derosne's earlier experiments, Serturner is generally credited with the discovery of morphine.

Within fifty years of its discovery, approximately twenty alkaloids were isolated, including codeine by Robiquet (1832) and papaverine by Merck (1848), and numerous derivatives including Dilaudid and heroin, Dionin, apocodeine and apomorphine. It was discovered that the alkaloids morphine and codeine were the active ingredients of opium, and were thus responsible for its widely known clinical effects. These active ingredients amount to approximately 25 per cent of opium by weight. The other 75 per cent consists of many unimportant substances, such as organic acids, gums and resins.*

Alkaloids

An alkaloid is a vegetable organic base with a nitrogenous ring in its molecule. Opium has two major and distinct classes of alkaloids: the phenanthrene group represented by morphine and codeine and the isoquinoline group represented by the important drug, papaverine. All the drugs in the phenanthrene group have a cross tolerance, so that, clinically, morphine and other derivatives in this group are interchangeable.

Papaverine and apomorphine, although non-addicting and non-narcotic, are included in the Harrison Narcotic Act because of their natural occurrence in opium.

The following table gives the major alkaloids of the two classes and their percentage in opium.[2, 3]

Group I, % in Opium	Group II, % in Opium
Phenanthrene	*Isoquinoline*
Morphine, 10.0 (3 to 23)	Papaverine, 1.0 (0.5 to 1.0)
Codeine, 0.5 (0.2 to .8)	Narcotine, 6.0 (0.7 to 10.0)
Thebaine, 0.2 (0.2 to 1.0)	Narceine, 0.3 (0.1 to 0.5)

Route of Administration

Opium, U.S.P., B.P., is absorbed through the lungs and through the gastrointestinal tract. Prepared in dosages of 1 grain (65 mg.), it is approved by the U. S. Pharmacopeia

---

*In a remarkable book entitled *Chemistry of the Opium Alkaloids*, published in 1932 (U. S. Public Health Service Supplement, No. 103, Public Health Reports), Dr. Lyndon Small, consultant in alkaloid chemistry to the United States Public Health Service, has painstakingly compiled the entire world literature on this subject. Dr. Small covers the historical discoveries throughout the years, and the controversy over the structural formulae.

though it is used much more frequently as a medical drug in Europe than in the United States. The following preparations are available: powdered opium; tincture of opium (laudanum); camphorated tincture of opium (paregoric); ipecac and opium powder (Dover's powder), and Pantopon.

Drug addicts are aware of the fact that in many states up to an ounce of paregoric can be bought without prescription and it is not uncommon for them to accumulate twenty or thirty ounces. Consumption in such large amounts can bring about a real addiction. I treated a 75 year old woman who had been addicted to paregoric only, ever since she had taken it as a young child for dysentery. Although it is still widely used in Europe, in America most physicians have found that bismuth is equally effective for diarrhea and much safer than any opiate drug.

Opium as a drug is considerably milder than its alkaloid, morphine. Even a boiled down, concentrated preparation of opium cannot compare, either in effect on the central nervous system or in addicting propensity, with morphine administered hypodermically. Oddly enough, the steady smoking of opium over a period of years in those countries where it is an accepted practice does not seem to produce addiction in many of the natives. However, a mild addiction can result from smoking opium in sufficient quantities.

The history of opium smoking as employed by the Chinese shows marked differences from that of morphine or heroin addiction. In the first place there is a pattern of self-limitation or restraint in opium smoking as practiced in countries where it is socially acceptable. It is common for natives of these countries to indulge in opium smoking one night a week, much as Americans may indulge in alcoholic beverages at a Saturday night party. Futhermore, opium smoking is neither largely confined to, nor necessarily identified with, the indigent or itinerant fringe but is just as socially ingrained in the country's ruling and wealthy classes.

The opium smoker reports an entirely different effect from that of the heroin addict: a state of inner peace and relaxation coupled with a desire for quiet, contemplative, social conversation. A Chinese and an American patient, both of upper-class family, have reported similar pleasurable impressions connected with this custom in the Orient. They indulged in the smoking of opium from one to three times a week on the average and had one pipe on each occasion. Opium smoking is usually done in a social situation. In fact, one patient reported that he had far less satisfaction from solitary smoking than from being one of a group. The conversation which flows during the smoking of opium is described as unhurried, thoroughly enjoyable and free from the usual competition and tension accompanying an interchange of ideas and thoughts. This state of relaxation does not preclude the enjoyment of friendly relationships within the group; in other words, subjective pleasurable experiences are not overpowering enough to make the individual smokers uninterested in their companions.

An Englishman who smoked opium while residing in the Orient—without becoming addicted, nor has he since relapsed to the use of any narcotic—shared many opium smoking sessions with his mistress. He described its effect of enhancing the sexual drive much as alcohol does, but in a far superior way. He found smoking opium more pleasurable than drinking alcohol because it was not accompanied by any diminution in muscular coordination. In general, opium smokers feel superior to addicts who inject morphine, and do not identify with them. Chinese families who accept opium smoking as part of their culture are mindful of its dangers much as we are mindful of the dangers of overindulgence in alcohol.

Stories of sexual orgies accompanying the smoking of opium are on the whole fallacious. In countries where it is socially accepted, people drop in to an establishment for an opium pipe much as the Frenchman drops into a bistro for a glass of wine. It is then apparent that the effects of smoking opium are similar to but far milder than those induced by hypodermically injected morphine or heroin. Even though the possibility of addiction is ever-present, it is a minor problem in the total picture of drug addiction in this country.

OPIUM DERIVATIVES

Morphine (with notes on Codeine)

Morphine and codeine, which occur naturally in opium, have a common structural basis—the phenanthrene group. Morphine is by all odds the most important opium derivative. For more than a century chemists have attempted without success to synthesize it. Dr. Small* gives several possible formulae but its exact structure is not yet known. The following structural formula corresponds closely to chemical properties of morphine.

$(C_{17} H_{19} NO_3)$

Morphine

The two important OH groups noted in the diagram are known as the phenolic and the alcoholic hydroxyls. Many of the other alkaloids have the same formula as morphine except that different radicals are substituted in one or both of these hydroxyl groups. For example, with codeine the one exception is that the phenolic OH is replaced by a methyl (CH_3) radical.

By checking the chemical formula against the varying degrees of analgesia observed clinically, it becomes apparent that the free phenolic OH in morphine is responsible for its increased action on the central nervous system—as an analgesic and as a respiratory depressant.

Morphine sulfate is white in color and has a bitter taste. It deteriorates with age and often takes on a brownish hue. As a mono-acid base, morphine is most commonly sold in the sulfate form, although it may be prepared as morphine acetate, morphine hydrochloride or morphine tartrate.

---

*See footnote, page 16.

Local Action. The opium alkaloids do not have any local anesthetic effects. Local use is not justified as they are not absorbed through the skin and in fact some of them irritate the skin and mucosa.

Absorption. Except from the skin, morphine and codeine are readily absorbed by the body—from the gastrointestinal tract as well as the subcutaneous tissues. This absorptive property makes intravenous injections usually unnecessary in medical practice, except possibly for cases of acute coronary thrombosis or others requiring emergency analgesia. Intravenous injections are for the most part confined to addicts who use this means to enhance morphine's excitatory effects.

Morphine circulating in the blood stream of a pregnant woman is absorbed by the fetus through the placental tissues. If the mother has been receiving morphine consistently, the fetus may become addicted and at birth the infant begins to experience withdrawal symptoms.

Detoxification and Excretion. Morphine leaves traces in all the body fluids, the gastric and intestinal juices, the saliva, the urine, and also in the feces. Although its clinical effects wear off within about four hours, the actual detoxification is spread over a twenty-four hour period. Of a given amount of morphine absorbed into the body, roughly 10 per cent is excreted and 90 per cent appears to be detoxified by the liver.

The above-mentioned 10 per cent of ingested morphine is excreted via all body fluids and the intestinal tract, although the urine is by far the biggest carrier. A nursing mother may addict her child through the morphine excreted in her milk.

Dosage. Morphine in the form of water-soluble salts for oral or hypodermic use is available in the following dosages: 1/12, 1/8, 1/6, 1/4, and 1/2 gr. (5, 8, 10, 15, 30 mg.)

A physician prescribing morphine gauges the dosage according to the patient's age and physical condition, as well as the level of excitability of his central nervous system. Women seem to have a low level of excitability, reacting more readily to morphine's toxic effects, and therefore usually require less of the drug for analgesia. The average adult dose is 1/6 to 1/4 grain. The average adult oral dose is 1/8 to 1/4 gr. For infants and young children the dosage is determined by their age and weight.[2]

Codeine (methyl morphine) $C_{18}H_{21}O_3N$

Codeine, a natural alkaloid of opium, is commonly prepared by substituting a methyl for morphine's phenolic OH. Although easily prepared from morphine in the laboratory, codeine has not as yet been converted back into morphine.

It was first isolated in 1832 by Robiquet, a French chemist, while he was extracting morphine from opium.[4] He at first considered it merely an impurity.

Codeine is approximately 20 per cent less effective as an analgesic than morphine and has only a fraction of morphine's depressant effect on the central nervous system and intestinal tract, but its stimulant and convulsive effects are greater. With codeine, 80 per cent of the drug is excreted in the urine as opposed to 10 per cent in the case of morphine.

Beyond question, codeine is an addicting drug, despite statements to the contrary in some pharmaceutical textbooks. Himmelsbach[5] describes codeine's tendency to produce physical dependence and tolerance. I had occasion to see a young veteran who had been picked up for stealing elixir of terpin hydrate and codeine. When alcohol was not available overseas, some of the GI's drank this common cough remedy which is always available. The young man unwittingly became tragically addicted. However, this elixir is rarely used by drug addicts because of its mild effects. It is important to realize that the maximum dosage of codeine is one grain. A larger amount is not pharmacologically justified since it may occasion restlessness and hyperexcitability.

Codeine, a soluble salt, is available in tablet form for oral and hypodermic use. The common preparations are codeine sulfate and the more readily water-soluble codeine phosphate. Dosages range from 1/4 grain to 1 grain, with the average dose 1/2 grain.

Heroin B.P. (diamorphine or acetomorphine)

When morphine is heated with acetic acid, both its alcoholic and phenohydroxyl groups become esterified, forming diacetylmorphine, or heroin. Heroin is therefore a synthetic alkaloid. Producing or importing heroin has been prohibited by law in the United States since 1925, so all traffic in this drug is carried on via the black market. As part of an international drug control program, it has been suggested that other countries also ban the production of heroin. It is highly desirable that all citizens and groups support the United Nations Commission on Narcotics in its untiring efforts toward this end. Many countries have already prohibited its manufacture, although it is still listed in the British Pharmacopoeia as diamorphine hydrochloride.

Heroin's effects are essentially the same as morphine's, except that there seem to be fewer side reactions. Its analgesic effects are superior, and it is a more powerful respiratory depressant than morphine. Its greater addiction liability makes the use of heroin both dangerous and unsound.

For most addicts, heroin is the drug of choice. It is smuggled into the United States from its original source in a pure form. Despite undergoing considerable watering down before it is sold to addicts in capsule or tablet form, its effect is still profound.

Heroin is practically always injected intravenously; in fact, the drug addict who uses it subcutaneously is a rarity. The intravenous route seems to induce greater and more intense satisfaction. Once an addict has used heroin, nothing else really satisfies him. He may have to resort to various opiates or synthetic drugs, but his activities are constantly directed toward obtaining his drug of choice.

Although the drug addict constantly desires and seeks heroin, with possession comes the simultaneous realization that he is no longer in control of his quest for pleasure and he becomes frightened. A young man who consulted me while addicted to methadone wanted to be withdrawn but had not fully made up his mind to undergo the necessary treatment. He rationalized his attitude by pointing out that he was able to work while on the drug. The next time this patient consulted me, six months later, he had been taking heroin for about two weeks and felt that he was already out of control. There was no question that he was desperate. He was quite willing to start withdrawal immediately, requested hospitalization and went through with the treatment.

It is difficult enough for a non-addict to handle the conflicting emotions aroused by a fierce desire and fear of the consequences when they are realized; it is vastly more so for an addict. On the one hand his desire for heroin is so strong that he will jeopardize his legal status and his very life to obtain it. On the other hand, he somehow realizes that giving in to this uncontrollable desire is fraught with danger, and he becomes frightened beyond words. Heroin precipitates these conflicting emotions to an extreme degree. In the absence of heroin, an addict considers morphine a good second best though it is only one-third as strong.

Dilaudid U.S.P. (dihydromorphinone hydrochloride)

The synthetic alkaloid Dilaudid is prepared by adding morphine to a strong acid in the presence of a platinum catalyst. This union forms a hydrogenated keto derivative which is called dihydromorphinone, first isolated and described in 1923.

As with every new synthetic alkaloid, Dilaudid was at first believed to be non-addicting. This belief persists, but it is without foundation in fact. Dilaudid is a favorite of many addicts, and physicians have reported their own experiences with it. A physician addicted to Dilaudid reported that it relieved the pain from his migraine headaches and allowed him to work without feeling at all drowsy or sleepy.

Dilaudid is approximately ten times as powerful an analgesic as morphine, but it has a minimal effect on sleep and causes much less nausea, vomiting and constipation than an equal amount of morphine.

Prepared for oral, hypodermic or rectal use, the average dose of Dilaudid is 1/32 to 1/16 grain (2–4 mg.). Since its analgesic effect is of shorter duration than morphine's, injections must be given more frequently, which of course increases its addiction potential—a factor of paramount importance in using this drug medically.

Metapon N.N.R. (7 methyl-dihydromorphinone hydrochloride)

Metapon is a synthetic drug derived from an alkaloid known as thebaine, occurring naturally in opium. Thebaine itself has no medical use; it is a convulsant poison.

Used in much the same way as morphine, Metapon's advantage lies in its effectiveness when taken orally. It is prepared for both oral and hypodermic use, and the average adult dose is 1/20 grain (3 mg.). Metapon is equally as addicting as the other opiates and is used interchangeably with them by drug addicts.

Dionin, Pantopon U.S.P.

Dionin (U.S.P.), ethyl morphine hydrochloride, is another synthetic derivative of morphine, and is considered to be merely a weaker form of codeine. Its major clinical use is in ophthalmology. Because of its irritant effect on the eye, a 2 per cent solution may be used to encourage hyperemia.

Pantopon, a proprietary drug, was widely acclaimed in its early days. It was believed to possess all of the therapeutic advantages of morphine without all of its toxic effects. Its claim to superiority on the grounds that its papaverine content counteracts the side effects of morphine, to which it is opposed, seems not to be justified; its percentage of papaverine is too small to cause much effect. In fact, its whole performance to date has not borne out its early promise. Pantopon is a purified form of opium containing all of the natural alkaloids in approximately their original percentages. It is popular with addicts because it is practically 50 per cent morphine. Its advantage over other opium preparations is that it is made up for hypodermic as well as for oral use.

Many other synthetic alkaloids have been developed in an effort to find a drug without addicting properties. But this goal is still unrealized, and all such drugs, including Dromoran, have been placed under Federal control. Other codeine derivatives are Eukodal (dihydroxycodeinone hydrochloride) and

Dicodide or Hycodan (dihydrohydrocodeinone bitartrate), both of which are much stronger than codeine.

Two derivatives of opium, apomorphine, an emetic as well as a potent central nervous system depressant, and papaverine, which relaxes smooth muscles, come under Federal control even though they are not addicting drugs.

SYNTHETIC OPIUM EQUIVALENTS

Among the synthetic opium equivalents are two major drugs, quite properly under Federal control: Demerol and the newer drug methadone, also known as Dolophine. That they have the same addicting propensity as the opiates is indicated by their widespread use among drug addicts. For some addicts, Demerol or methadone is actually the drug of choice.

Demerol (meperidine, Dolantin, isonipecaine) (1 methyl, 4 phenyl-piperdine 4 carboxylic acid ethyl hydrochloride)

Demerol, synthesized in 1939, was hailed as a non-addicting analgesic with the potency of morphine. But many individuals medically addicted to Demerol eventually found themselves at Lexington for treatment. Demerol as an addicting drug was described by H. Weider[6] in 1946. Its effects are similar to those of morphine but of shorter duration. It has a depressant action on smooth muscles. Demerol is sold in 2 cc. ampules of 100 mg. each, and also in tablet form for oral use. The average adult dose is 50 to 100 mg.

Several new compounds in the meperidine family have been isolated and their addiction liabilities studied.[7] Of these, Keto-Bemidone is found to be superior to Demerol. It is distributed in Europe, but since it is believed to be even more addicting than heroin,[8] it will undoubtedly be banned in the United States.

Methadone (Amidon, Dolophine, "10820," Adanon)

Methadone is a new synthetic analgesic. Following World War II, chemists of the allied countries came upon this drug in the German laboratories where it was discovered. Like Demerol, it was welcomed as the long-awaited non-addicting analgesic. But research at Lexington proved otherwise: It differs from morphine only in that the withdrawal symptoms are milder and do not set in immediately upon withdrawal of the drug. Addicts readily accept it as a substitute for morphine or heroin.

Addicts consider methadone less satisfactory than morphine because its euphoric effects are not as great, and with repeated administration it tends to have a depressant effect. It is successfully substituted for morphine in the withdrawal treatment which is recommended in a later chapter. As to potency, 1 mg. of methadone can be substituted for 3 mg. of morphine. Methadone is prepared commerically in ampules, powder and tablet forms, for oral or hypodermic use. The average adult dose is 1/12 gr. (5 mg.).

OPIATE POISONING

Although drug addicts can develop sufficient tolerance to enable them to take eight times their normal dosage of drugs without ill effects, it is nevertheless possible for them to take a lethal dose. The death of countless drug addicts is no doubt attributable to stronger dosages of drugs than they had become used to. Inasmuch as black market drugs are diluted, addicts depending on this source do not really know precisely how much they are taking.

Severe opiate poisoning results in coma. The heart rate and the blood pressure are lowered. Breathing is shallow and the skin is cold. Respiratory depression causes marked cyanosis and subsequent asphyxia.

If the opiates have been taken orally, the stomach contents should be immediately pumped out. The free passage of air should be insured by keeping the tongue depressed. Nalline (N-allylnormorphine) evokes an immediate response.

Nalline (N-allylnormorphine)

Nalline is a new drug, derived from codeine, which has been developed by the Merck laboratories. Up to now it has been used mainly in research at Lexington.

This drug's amazing properties make it suitable for clinical use as a specific antidote for poisoning (respiratory depression) by heroin, morphine, methadone, Dilaudid and Pantopon. Lacking Nalline, the physician should use the next best means —prompt administration of oxygen and stimulants.

At long last, it seems that the medical profession has a specific and reliable means of determining whether a patient is addicted to drugs. When individuals who have been regularly receiving morphine are injected with Nalline, withdrawal symptoms set in within one-half hour. They closely resemble the symptoms produced by the abrupt withdrawal of morphine: lacrimation, dilation of pupils, nausea, twitching, vomiting, diarrhea, etc. The drug addict has his own term for Nalline— Babo, "the stuff that really cleans you out."

The average dose which will produce these results is 5 mg.

This drug is proving to be an invaluable aid both clinically and in research on the mechanism of addiction. It should be a great boon to the courts dealing with drug addicts as well as to the hospitals where detection is the first step toward coping with medically induced addiction. (Further discussion of Nalline will be found in Chapter III, page 51, and Chapter VI, page 110.)

DANGEROUS STIMULANTS

Cocaine U.S.P. (*cocaine hydrochloride*)

Cocaine is a natural alkaloid obtained from the leaves of the *Erythroxylon coca* tree. Known as the "divine plant of the Incas," this tree is native to South America and Mexico. For centuries inhabitants of these countries have claimed that chewing its leaves brought them relief from hunger and fatigue.

Chemically, cocaine is an ester of benzoic acid and a nitrogenous base. Structurally it resembles other synthetic local anesthetics.

Its pharmacological action is a stimulation of the central nervous system and, on local application, a blocking of sensory nerve conduction. Pharmacological dependence or evidence of tolerance has not yet been determined, inasmuch as research dealing with cocaine is limited. However, the general opinion is that any dependency on the drug is psychological rather than chemical.

Cocaine produces a wild euphoric excitement which may be accompanied by visual hallucinations. The cocaine user experiences a feeling of great mental and physical power. At the same time this drug seems to foster paranoidal feelings; the user feels threatened; he is sure that people are "out to get him." The resulting persecution complex may spur him to retaliative violence and homicidal attempts. These well-known psychotic effects deter addicts from using cocaine in its pure state and they admit to being fearful of its consequences. The unpleasant effects are mitigated by combining cocaine with heroin or other opiates—a combination called a "speed ball" which many addicts find highly desirable.

Addicts may inject cocaine or sniff the powder, commonly known as "snow." Injections of cocaine cause characteristic multiple abscesses which immediately reveal this particular addiction. Perforation of the nasal septum may result from repeatedly sniffing the drug. Addicts have been known to use from 30 to 60 grains of cocaine daily for short periods,[9] but 6 grains is the average dosage used by addicts.

With cocaine there seems to be scant evidence of any pharmacological dependence, but the unquestioned psychological dependence produces the same purposive behavior common to addicts of other narcotics: they will go to any lengths to obtain it. Cocaine users eagerly solicit the job of cleaning physicians' offices on the chance of picking up some applicators that have been used for cocaine. Relatively unpopular in the addict world, cocaine is not a brisk black market item.

Physician addicts who have easy access to cocaine frequently use it in conjunction with other narcotics. Newspaper accounts of addicts who have violently resisted arrest suggest that they were on cocaine. When a well-known jazz artist was arrested for possessing narcotics, she was reported to have tried to shoot and to run over the arresting officers. She was clearly psychotic at the time from the habitual use of cocaine.

Cocaine is absorbed through the mucous membranes and produces a loss of the sense of touch and an immunity to pain.

It had a long vogue in ophthalmology, where it was used to deaden the exquisite sensitiveness of the cornea. Because of its deleterious effects, it is gradually being replaced for this purpose by synthetic drugs.

In medical practice, cocaine is neither used internally nor injected. It is sold in solution for local use: 1–4 per cent.for the eye and 10–20 per cent for the nose. It has been rejected as a cortical stimulant because dangerous mental toxic reactions often follow.

Cocaine poisoning is quite common. Many individuals have a susceptibility to dosages as small as 1/3 gr. (20 mg.). In cases of acute cocaine poisoning, the patient may pass quickly from convulsions to coma to death. Among the preliminary symptoms are unrestrained laughter, talkativeness, vomiting, irregular pulse and convulsions, each phase following in rapid succession. Treatment of the toxic effects of cocaine consists of intravenous injections of barbiturates. Barbiturates may be given by mouth, one-half hour before the cocaine, so that the two effects coincide and preclude cocaine's toxic effects.

Marijuana

Marijuana is a drug derived from the flowering tops of a variety of hemp plants (*Cannabis americana*). For many centuries up to the present time it has been used as an intoxicant in China, India, Africa, Europe and more recently in the Americas. The use of marijuana dates back to 3000 B.C. and in many lands it is as customary an indulgence as the American cocktail. It has many names in various lands, among them hashish, ganga and manzoul. The preparation itself varies slightly in different countries, along with the form of administration. It may be taken by mouth, combined with sweet tasting liquids or incorporated in food, or, as in America, it may be smoked in the form of cigarettes. Several countries which have allowed free traffic in marijuana are beginning to pass restrictive laws governing its use.

American addicts refer to marijuana as "tea" and in cigarette form as "reefers." It is particularly popular among jazz musicians,[10] who feel that it enhances their playing skill, and with adolescent jazz enthusiasts who feel that it enhances their joy and perceptiveness in listening.

There has been considerable controversy over its inclusion in the Harrison Narcotic Act, inasmuch as it is not a narcotic and there is no evidence of physical dependence or abnormal tolerance. As with all stimulants, some measure of control is desirable, especially in view of its world-wide increase in use.

The effects of marijuana resemble those of alcohol and are just as numerous and varied. Subjectively, its reactions range from nothing through a whole gamut: nausea, drowsiness, exhilaration, overexcitement, and impairment or loss of judgment. A number of authorities greatly exaggerate the drug's effects; by publicizing its so-called horrors they can justify the severe penalties imposed upon marijuana users, whose legal sentences may be as severe as those meted out to drug addicts. Depending upon the court handing out the sentence, the marijuana smoker may even receive a maximum penalty. Although hashish has long been bracketed with psychosis in China, I have seen only one marijuana smoker in psychosis— and a seemingly transient one at that.

Marijuana is primarily a social problem, not a medical one. This drug does not follow the normal pattern of a stimulant. Adolescents find it daring and exciting to try anything forbidden, and unfortunately their pursuit of marijuana invariably brings them into contact with drug addicts. After marijuana it is simple enough to introduce them to heroin or morphine—often the one-two-three sequence of addiction to these more potent drugs. Because of this connection with drug peddlers, ruling out marijuana along with opiates is the sensible legal resort. On the other hand, to build up propaganda for marijuana as a corrupting drug is to falsify the picture; its ill effects are equalled if not exceeded by those of alcohol.

Marijuana users report a variety of effects, the most common of which is a period of euphoria lasting about two hours and accompanied by moderate sexual stimulation. Control subjects in experiments have reported a sense of time distortion— a feeling of everything slowing down, with no need to rush. Toxic symptoms include drowsiness, tachycardia and nausea.

Marijuana cigarettes sell for fifty cents to one dollar each. They resemble a loosely-packed, king-size cigarette. Here again we find a socially utilized intoxicant, seldom if ever used in solitude. Groups who gather for a "tea party" smoke their reefers while listening to music and conversing. They report sexual stimulation but there is little acting upon their feelings. They seldom dance but merely smoke, listen to music and discuss it somewhat seriously.

Recently, a new activity has become popular among marijuana smokers. A group will set out in a car, listening to music on the radio and smoking reefers. As a rule they drive very slowly and aimlessly with no goal or sense of hurrying and play the radio very loudly. Despite this pattern, it must be remembered that marijuana, like alcohol, impairs the judgment, and it is quite possible that automobile accidents involving teenagers may occur while the driver is under the influence of this drug, just as they may result from alcoholic sprees.

The smoking of a marijuana cigarette is somewhat of a ritual. The smoker inhales noisily, taking in air along with the drug. This mixture is held in the lungs as long as possible, to allow complete absorption. One cigarette may have little effect and so it is followed by a second or more, inhaled in the same way, until the desired effect is achieved.

A synthetic marijuana substance has been used experimentally with patients at Lexington. It is significant that addicts did not enjoy participating in this experiment and expressed relief when it was over.

Peyote (mescaline)

Peyote, frequently confused with marijuana, is actually from an entirely different source—the button-like top of two species of the cactus: *Lophophora williamsii* and *Lophophora lewinii*. The active ingredient of peyote is the alkaloid mescaline.

When mescaline is given to normal subjects it produces a variety of central nervous system effects including brilliantly colored visual hallucinations in the form of geometric patterns.[11, 11a]

Peyote is used exclusively by American Indians of the Southwest as part of their religious ritual. The technicolor hallucinations are interpreted as part of a religious experience. There is no evidence that peyote is habit forming, but it is included in the roster of dangerous drugs under Federal control.

Benzedrine (amphetamine sulfate)

Benzedrine and Dexedrine, both dangerous drugs, are properly considered in a general discussion of narcotics. The widespread use of Benzedrine, "Benny" in the parlance of addicts, followed in the wake of publicity that it increases the work output and is at the same time exhilarating.

The consumption of Benzedrine rapidly took on such proportions that radio and television comedians were soon referring to it on their programs and the average listener knew what they were talking about. In its early days, physicians prescribed this drug for everything from obesity to low back pain. Continued use made its toxic properties known and it is now more cautiously handled in the profession. The toxic effects include insommnia, anorexia, restlessness, irritability, tachycardia, visual and auditory hallucinations and paranoic delusions.[12]

Individuals have been known to take ten to twenty times the dosage recommended by their physicians. Tolerance to Benzedrine can go even higher, reaching 1500 mg. daily, contrasted with the average dose of 5–10 mg.[13] Its intoxicant effects reduce addicts to sleeplessness, but they can use barbiturates to induce sleep. Thus their physical energies are derived from chemicals: they sleep on sedatives and work on stimulants.

A married woman, mother of two children, was referred by her physician to a psychiatrist when she complained of increasing irritability, often culminating in real rages. It developed that she had become extremely depressed and fatigued during her second pregnancy. Her physician prescribed Benzedrine and she used it for three months with relief of her symptoms. She was able to function normally for several years, but a few months prior to her consultation with the psychiatrist, she had again become depressed. Since Benzedrine had helped

her through a similar period, she had the prescription refilled
and was soon taking approximately 30 mg. daily. This is an
example of accidental or unconscious addiction. The patient
retained the memory of Benzedrine's effects for years; when she
had a similar depression she took the drug without consulting
a physician and rapidly became addicted.

Addicts consider Benzedrine a highly desirable stimulant.
For many years the manner in which they made use of Benzedrine in prisons was a mystery. It was found that they chewed
or even swallowed the saturated paper in the Benzedrine in-
halators. Incidentally, manufacturers are now substituting a
milder drug in the inhalator. The euphoric effect of Benzedrine
is accompanied by a release from troubles and worries so that
it has decided advantages under proper handling.

BARBITURATES

Only within the past seven years or so has the United
States been alerted to the serious addicting properties of barbiturates. Although this fact has since then received wide
publicity, the amount of barbiturates still being prescribed in
this country constitutes a serious threat to our national health.
There has been no question of the addictive nature of barbiturates since Dr. H. Isbell made his first experimental research study on this problem at Lexington, using patients who
had been previously addicted to opiates.[14] The results proved
conclusively that tolerance to barbiturates develops in varying
degrees, and furthermore that a definite abstinence syndrome
follows the abrupt withdrawal of barbiturates.

Barbiturate consumption has more than doubled in the
last ten years, but the lower figures for 1954 may indicate a
trend downward from a peak consumption. Barbiturates have
largely been brought under state control, and the law requires
that each purchaser present a physician's prescription, which in
most states cannot be refilled. Even so, many a pharmacist still
dispenses unlimited amounts of barbiturates without prescription, risking an investigation which would mean losing his
license. It is impossible to estimate with any degree of accuracy
the number of chronic barbiturate users and barbiturate ad-

dicts in the United States, but it unquestionably exceeds the number of drug addicts by many times. It is fortunate that barbiturates are not included in the Harrison Narcotic Act. The great demand would create a black market of proportions impossible to control, and overnight perhaps a million persons would be criminals in the eyes of the law. The wisest and best solution seems to be to apprise the physician of the inherent danger in prescribing barbiturates indiscriminately, rather than to limit his authority to prescribe them.

Barbiturates are contraindicated in the case of any addiction-prone individuals, *particularly alcoholics.* Alcoholics Anonymous urges physicians not to give any barbiturate to an alcoholic as a sedative. In attempting to control their drinking, many A. A. members have become seriously addicted to barbiturates. This can be a case of frying-pan-into-fire, for alcoholism and barbiturate addiction have marked common characteristics.

The barbiturate addict is usually unkempt in appearance. With little motor control over gross or fine movements, he may have a staggering gait, and poorly articulated speech. Emotionally he is likely to veer between extremes: one moment warm and friendly and the next erupting into violence, perhaps over a slight disagreement with someone. His judgment is impaired and, like the alcoholic, he appears to be indulging in inner fantasies rather than reacting to outer reality.

Barbiturate addiction and opiate addiction present quite different clinical pictures. Dr. Wikler describes this difference in psychological terms: opiates reduce the primary needs of hunger and sex, whereas barbiturates "impair the ability of the individual to suppress patterns of behavior which are developed in relation to the active gratification of both primary and secondary needs."[13]

Barbiturate addiction builds up in easy stages. The patient usually begins with a prescribed dosage. Instead of resting in bed until the drug works, he sits up and reads until it "knocks him out." While reading, a drowsy euphoria slowly envelops him, replacing his anxiety with a sense of well being. When he subsequently experiences anxiety or tension in his work, he is likely to recall the effect of sleeping pills and take one during the daytime *with no intention of sleeping.* This marks the second step in his addiction. Within a relatively short time he may be taking 4 grains a day. With the building up of tolerance comes the usual need for ever increasing doses, and it is not unusual to find an addict taking from 15 to 30 grains of a barbiturate daily.

The abrupt withdrawal of barbiturates is followed by a severe abstinence syndrome, a majority of the addict-patients developing tonic-clonic seizures and psychosis. The management of barbiturate withdrawal is discussed fully in Chapter VII.

Although hospitalization is generally necessary for barbiturate withdrawal, many patients can be taken off during the course of intensive psychiatric treatment. This can be accomplished without direct pressure but with ample educative discussion of barbiturates. The patient when ready begins to reduce his intake of barbiturates, and he gradually eliminates them altogether. After six months of intensive therapy, a 46 year old male patient who was taking twenty-four $1\frac{1}{2}$ grain capsules of Nembutal a day took himself off the drug within one month's time. One week after he had been free of drugs he experienced a "blackout" on the street and remained unconscious for several hours. He suffered no further ill effects. The "blackout" undoubtedly resulted from too rapid a reduction. It is interesting to note that the patient went off drugs so quickly that his body had trouble adapting to the new order.

Although psychiatric treatment is fairly successful in the treatment of barbiturate addiction, Danny Carlson, founder of Narcotics Anonymous, has found barbiturate addicts perhaps the most resistant of all when it comes to voluntary hospitalization.

When their drug of choice is not available, narcotic addicts will use barbiturates injected intravenously for heightened effect. These drugs, actually prepared for oral use, cause large necrotic abscesses to appear. Frequently the physician sees an addict whose body is deeply pitted all over with the scars of these abscesses.

It is important for the physician to keep in mind that when barbiturates are given primarily for insomnia, alcoholism, hyperexcitability, nervousness and acute depression rather than for actual pain, these drugs are being used solely for symptoms produced by emotional disturbances. The real disorder is emotional, the barbiturates being used to attack its manifold symptoms. In defending the prescribing of barbiturates to a patient who later became addicted, a physician said, "What else could I do? She was obviously hysterical. She hadn't slept for a week after breaking off with her boy friend." His argument has a certain validity, for there is no question that fatigue weakens a person's ability to cope with stress situations. On the other hand, barbiturates, like opiates, may launch the patient on a way of life instead of providing him with a temporary crutch until he can safely walk unaided.

Forewarned, the physician may mitigate this distress without resorting to any strong sedative. Futhermore, the average sedative dose is approximately twice as strong as is necessary to insure the average patient a good night's sleep. In dealing with specific complaints of insomnia and anxiety, I have found that discussing with the patient his symptoms—in themselves alarming to him—may take the place of medication. The patient reacts to his lack of sleep with panic, and his panic becomes more of a problem than the lack of sleep itself. It is commonly believed that some horrible physical upset or deterioration will result from a lack of sleep; patients frequently express fear of going insane or having a heart attack. The physician's knowledge of the symptoms and his ability to assess them properly figure at this point. Assuring the patient that such fears are groundless will dissipate his gnawing anxiety and bring him great relief.

The physician can allay the patient's anxiety about sleeplessness by telling him that one does not have to lose consciousness in order to rest, that one can obtain sufficient relaxation to function adequately by simply lying in bed, even tossing, instead of getting up, moving about or reading.

It is hoped that the foregoing discussion of barbiturates has made clear how important is the physician's task of specifically instructing and warning his patients about these drugs.

A realistic description of the dangers lurking in sleeping pills might help to make the patient both temperate and cautious, so that he would be willing to lose an occasional night's sleep rather than risk addiction. In any event the patient must be cautioned to remain in bed after he has taken the pills. It is well to give him specific instruction covering the usual contingencies: he should first have something to eat, bathe, get into bed and read a while if he likes, *then* take the sedative, turning off the light immediately. He will then not be awake to feel any euphoric effects from the drug. I have never known of a person to become addicted to barbiturates in a hospital, no doubt because the lights are turned off right after the nurse makes rounds with the night medication. Under these circumstances the patient can do nothing but cooperate with the action of the drug.

REFERENCES

1. Sertürner: Trommsdorff's Journal der Pharmazie, *13:* 234, 1805.
2. Goodman, L. and Gilman, A.: The Pharmacological Basis of Therapeutics. New York, Macmillan, 1941.
3. Davison, F. R.: Handbook of Materia Medica. St. Louis, C. V. Mosby, 1949.
4. Robiquet: Ann. Chim. Phys. *51:* 225, 1832
5. Himmelsbach, C. K.: Studies of addiction liability of codeine, J. A. M. *103:* 1420, 1934.
6. Wieder, H.: Addiction to meperidine hydrochloride (demerol hydrochloride). J. A. M. A. *132:* 1066, 1946.
7. Isbell, H.: The addiction liability of some derivatives of meperidine. J. Pharmacol & Exper. Therap. *97:* 182, 1949.
8. Maurer, D. W., and Vogel, V. H.: Narcotics and Narcotic Addiction. Springfield, C. C Thomas, 1954.
9. Kolb, L: Cocaine addiction. In Cecil's Textbook of Medicine, ed 7. Philadelphia, Saunders, 1948.
10. Aldrich, C. K.: The effects of a synthetic cannabis-like compound on musical talent as measured by the Seashore test. Pub. Health Rep. *59:* 431, 1944.
11. Hoch, P. H.: Experimentally produced psychoses. Am. J. Psychiat. *107:* 607, 1951.
11a. Cholden, Louis (ed.): Lysergic Acid Diethylamide and Mescaline in Experimental Psychiatry. New York, Grune & Stratton, 1956.
12. Norman, J., and Shea, J. T.: Acute hallucinosis as a complication of addiction to amphetamine sulfate. New England. J. Med. *223:* 270, 1945.
13. Wikler, A.: Drug addiction. In Tice's Practice of Medicine. Hagerstown, W. F. Prior Co., 1953.
14. Isbell, H., et al.: Chronic barbiturate intoxication. An experimental study. Arch. Neurol. & Psychiat. *64:* 1, 1950.

III. Physiology

GENERAL REMARKS

How CAN AN ADDICT survive what is ordinarily considered a lethal dose of drugs? What physical and psychological experiences does he have under these conditions? Is it true that addiction is purely psychological? Are withdrawal symptoms psychological? And if not, how can they be explained? Does the addict have a different metabolism from the non-addict? These questions are uppermost in the minds of those attempting to understand and cope with the problem of drug addiction. We shall try to find the answers thus far advanced by reviewing the research which has been going on over the years.

Research on drug addiction has from the start followed many paths. A number of the early researchers believed the answer to addiction was to be found in metabolic studies, and their efforts were directed toward proving that an increasing destruction of morphine goes on in the body, thus enabling the addict to take ever-increasing doses of the drug. When the development of psychiatric and psychological techniques had increased our knowledge of human behavior, an effort was made to correlate addiction with a certain type of personality. Then, with the development of highly skilled techniques for brain surgery, the focus changed to the central nervous system. By determining what areas of the brain were involved in making a person succumb to addiction it was hoped to establish, by reasoning backward, what areas of the brain were affected during the process of addiction.

Much of the research of these investigators has been fruitful, but there are large uninvestigated or superficially investigated areas; for example, the relationship of addiction to the endocrine glands, as demonstrated by the cessation of menstruation in the female addict, or the reasons why there is such an alarmingly low eosinophile count during withdrawal. Similarly,

exploration of the phenomenon of relapse must clearly go beyond the purely psychologically causative factors, for there is
now conclusive clinical evidence that addicts who have long
been off drugs still experience a true physiological craving and
need for them.

Only within the last decade has addiction been defined in
terms of clinical phenomena which can be subjected to scientific methodology. The literature is full of intuitional generaliz-
ing and theorizing—as varied as the explanations for the fall
of the Roman Empire wherein all of the groups concerned
ascribed the debacle to different causes, according to their own
background and orientation.

As in all scientific research, the description and definition
of the entire problem to be investigated is of paramount importance. The most inclusive definition of drug addiction I
have found is that of Dr. A. Wikler:

> "Drug addiction may be said to exist when the behavior of an
> individual is determined to a considerable extent by the avail-
> ability, for his use, of chemical agents which are harmful to him-
> self, society, or both."[14]

This definition would indicate four different areas for investigation. These are:
1. Research into behavioristic changes caused by narcotics.
2. Research into the chemical structure of narcotics.
3. Research into the sites of drug action within the body.
4. Research into the sociological aspects of addiction.

It can readily be seen that these are large and distinctly
separate areas; and therein lies the difficulty, from a research
standpoint. Each field has its own methods of investigation, its
own special terminology, its own frame of reference and criteria
for evaluation. Together they cover the fields of psychology and
psychiatry, chemistry, neurophysiology, pharmacology and
sociology.

The worker attempting to evaluate the results of research
on this subject should be warned of two pitfalls: (1) the tendency to believe he has found *the* answer to drug addiction

based on data gleaned from only one of the fields of investigations; and (2) the tendency to correlate data prematurely.

U. S. Public Health Service Hospital at Lexington. Before spanning the years to give the highlights of early and recent research, I should like to describe the laboratories responsible for much of our present knowledge. The first important, large scale research was started in 1935, when the Federal Government built a hospital at Lexington, Kentucky, exclusively for the purpose of studying and treating drug addiction. Lexington as a research center remains unique throughout the world. From its thorough research, under the able direction of Dr. Harris Isbell, has come the bulk of our knowledge about drug addiction. The material in this chapter has been drawn largely from the thinking and research of Dr. Abraham Wikler, experimental neuropsychiatrist at Lexington. An excellent detailed summary of the psychological and neurophysiological aspects of the subject can be found in his text *Opiate Addiction.*

The laboratory takes up a large area in the Lexington prison-hospital. A person entering one of the units is immediately impressed by the friendly relaxed atmosphere, with patients and staff members working side by side. Patients are employed to help in various capacities—to care for animals used in experiments, and so on. A number of rooms are devoted to the chemical analysis of drugs as well as the chemical detection tests in body fluids. Other rooms contain complete neurophysiological equipment to carry out research on the central and peripheral nervous systems. The electroencephalography room is set up for animals as well as for humans. Individual offices are available for interviewing patients and giving them psychological tests.

In one wing, leading out from a large dormitory hall, there are a number of single rooms, each equipped with a bed and dresser. Patients who are taking part in experiments live in these rooms sometimes for months at a time. This unique 24-hour-a-day study plan enables the staff to know the patient while he is off drugs—to observe his personal habits, his usual daily routine, how he functions on a job, and the normal fluctuations in his personality. Then when the patient is experimentally addicted, his total behavior can be observed under as "natural" conditions as can be arranged. It should be noted that the attitude of the laboratory research staff carries no moral censure nor does it reflect the restrictive and punitive attitude which is common to any hospital-prison.

Remarkable in itself is the fact that this laboratory has a plenteous supply of human beings who can safely be used in studying addiction. These human guinea pigs are patients from the general hospital who volunteer to take part in the research. A majority of the patients are eager to volunteer for they are promised a reward or "pay-off" in the form of a shot of morphine to be taken in any way they prefer, regardless of the outcome of the experiment. These patients are usually serving three to five year sentences and would not, of course, be chosen for experimental addiction if they were soon to be released.

The laboratory has a large animal section for dogs, cats, monkeys, etc. A well-known obstacle in neurophysiology is keeping animals alive following decorticate or spinal operative procedures. In fact, it is difficult enough to keep a decorticate animal alive long enough for a class demonstration in medical school. However, the constant around-the-clock nursing care provided by the prisoner-patients has made it possible to keep alive difficult surgical preparations for weeks or even months. The laboratory team, consisting of a psychiatrist, an experimental neuropsychiatrist, a chemist, a psychologist, a hematologist and a physiologist can thus conduct valuable continuing experiments.

EARLY RESEARCH

In the 16th century, before opium was widely known in China, the Europeans were well aware of its effectiveness in relieving pain and controlling diarrhea. Crude opium was refined into solutions and tinctures. The Swiss physician and alchemist, Paracelsus (1493–1541), is credited with the development and popularization of opium in the form of laudanum, which was believed to be a specific cure for various diseases.

The beginning of the 19th century marked the isolation and development of the first alkaloid of opium—morphine (1803). Isolation of the other alkaloids, including codeine and papaverine, followed in rapid succession, and heroin was discovered in the late nineties. Research at this time centered on the chemistry of the opium alkaloids and the search for a drug possessing the therapeutic properties of opium without being habit forming.

To appreciate how recent is our knowledge of morphine and drug addiction, one has only to read what the medical experts on narcotics from 1918 to 1920 had to say. Drug addiction as a clinical entity was known but nothing was known of the mechanisms and processes involved. Withdrawal symptoms were considered largely hysterical, and suggestions to relieve them ranged from high colonics to violent emetics.

The foundations of our modern research were laid in the twenties with studies centered on the phenomenon of the addict's amazing tolerance for drugs. Medical research was concentrated on the new, rich field of body metabolism, and it was natural that early researchers in drug addiction should accept the idea that tolerance is due to a metabolic dysfunction.

Studies were undertaken to determine whether the addict was better able than others to excrete morphine, or to destroy it in the body, or whether he was, perhaps, less able to absorb it. But this line of research received a severe blow in 1932 with the report of a careful study using animals. It seems that there was no significant difference in the amount of morphine excreted in the urine of addicted and non-addicted animals.[1]

These negative findings led to the emergence of a pharmacological theory, the Dual Action theory,[9] which postulates that morphine has two distinct pharmacological actions on the central nervous system: a depressant action and an excitatory action (not to be confused with the subjective experience of the patient). Upon injection of morphine, the excitatory action becomes masked by the depressant, but the excitatory action is longer lasting, thus allowing for a greater tolerance to additional morphine.

The Cellular Tolerance theory, which became popular in the thirties, was based on the supposition that the cells of the central nervous system become hyperirritable as a result of morphine addiction. Therefore they require, and hence can tolerate, more morphine to reduce their state to one of relative equilibrium.

In 1940, Oberst[2] revived the metabolic studies and found that morphine is excreted in the urine in two forms: free and bound. His work under improved methods of detection substantiated the earlier theory that a metabolic acceleration allows the addict to destroy morphine, and thus reopened research along this line.

THE EFFECT OF A SINGLE DOSE OF MORPHINE

Morphine, the principal and most widely used derivative of opium, is the drug used in experimental procedures unless otherwise indicated. It would be ridiculous to assume that a full understanding of the problem of addiction lies in even the most exhaustive examination of the physiological effects of a single dose of morphine. However, such effects constitute a firm basis for our knowledge.

Individuals of all personality types have been tested following the injection of a single dose of morphine. Although subjective central nervous system experiences may vary widely, they may also be very similar among certain addicts. These individual reactions range from none to the full toxic effects: dizziness, drowsiness, nausea and vomiting. Many people have a feeling of inner relaxation, a sense of well being, after a shot of morphine. Others experience a definite exhilaration throughout the body. This type of reaction, well known to most drug addicts, is the thrill which they call a "kick" or a "bang." Because this exhilarating or orgastic reaction was so commonly observed in addicts, researchers came to the conclusion that a single dose of morphine evoked two basically different reactions. Those people who experienced pleasure, whether or not they were drug addicts, were considered prone to addiction; those who experienced no reaction were considered to be safe from addiction. This distinction has not weathered the test of time. Staff workers who have on occasion acted as control subjects while doing research on morphine found that their initial negative reactions changed after repeated experiments; they began to feel certain euphoric effects from the drug. At Lexington, where staff members are occasionally used as controls in testing the reactions of drugs, precautionary measures include a long spacing between drug administration.

Observation of positive reactions in so-called "addiction-safe" personalities has led to the conclusion that it is both fallacious and dangerous to assume that any individual, regardless of his education and training, could not become addicted. The explanation is a simple one: no matter how well he is functioning in society, there is probably no one so free of tension, so immune to anxiety, that morphine will not in time have a pleasant effect on him.

Studies of the subjective reactions of addicts to a single dose of morphine reveal that many of them experience a feeling of exhilaration, akin to an orgasm discharged in the abdominal region. It is entirely possible that the intensity of this pleasure exceeds any pleasure known to non-addicts. This possibility occurred to me as I watched an addict at Lexington receive his "pay-off" of one-quarter grain of morphine, after finishing his part in a research experiment. He chose to have the morphine injected in his neck vein, and as he sat there a slow flush crept over his body. He rubbed his head and his arms in an expression of pure joy and said, "This is why men go to prison, and it's worth it."

Morphine further acts on the central nervous system by producing a state of relaxation which may go over into sleep—referred to by addicts as "being on the nod." This sleep is deep and frequently dreamless.

CHANGES IN MENTAL CAPACITY AS REFLECTED IN WORK

There is no appreciable difference in an individual's performance after a single dose of morphine. His judgment, reasoning and skill are apparently not impaired.

What happens to the mind of an addicted person? It has been held that all addicts undergo mental deterioration and exhibit the disorientation and cloudy sensorium of the alcoholic. But researchers observing the daily work habits and personal behavior of individuals who have become addicted say that the change is at first slight. If no work was required of the patients observed at Lexington, they tended to give in to the relaxation and drowsiness which inevitably followed the shot. Reading, conversation and eating became less and less important to them; they seemed simply to be living for the next shot. Nevertheless, they could carry on their work if they were obliged to do so. Contrary to popular opinion, morphine's effects on the central nervous system are not such as to interfere with the addict's ability to work in society nor yet to lessen his moral judgment.

The criminal acts committed by addicts result from their need to obtain drugs rather than from any organic mental deterioration. There is no evidence that addicts are essentially criminal and therefore should be controlled by harsher laws, as has been suggested by a probation officer.[11]

Experiments show that addicted animals exhibit morphine-oriented behavior. Spragg[10] addicted chimpanzees and then offered them a choice of food or drugs (1) when they had been fed and injected, (2) when they were hungry and needed an injection, (3) when they were hungry but had been given an injection, and (4) when they had been fed but needed an injection. Their choices as well as their behavior were surprisingly similar to those of humans under the same circumstances. The animals chose food only under conditions (1) and (3) and chose drugs under conditions (2) and (4). Furthermore, while undergoing withdrawal symptoms, the animals tried in every way to get an injection. They would bend over in the position they assumed during injection; they would become excited when a syringe was shown to them. Such purposive, drug-oriented behavior apparently does not require a criminal mind.

BODILY FUNCTION

Sexuality

Accumulated data disproves the fictional and so-called factual accounts associating drug addicts with maniacal sexual orgies. Although the exact mechanism of morphine's action on the reproductive system is unknown, there is sufficient evidence to show that it diminishes the sexual appetite. Sexual difficulties invariably occur when either the husband or wife becomes addicted, due to his or her complete lack of interest in sex, which frequently persists even when the addict is off drugs. A male addict, having been in prison for two or three years, has no difficulty in answering the question of whether he would rather have a luscious girl or a shot of morphine. Without hesitation he invariably names morphine as his choice.

A sufficiently large number of female addicts report cessation of menstruation during addiction to suggest that drugs act on the endocrine glands. However, ovulation must continue since pregnancies do occur. There is no evidence that fertility in the male is impaired.

Although I have never seen a case where addiction enhanced the sexual drive to abnormal heights, a few patients have described their sexual life as normal while on drugs. These patients frequently give a history of anxiety concerning the sexual act and say that morphine enables them to obtain sexual satisfaction without accompanying anxiety.

Gastrointestinal Tract

Morphine's effects on the stomach—allaying or reducing hunger sensations—are not mediated through the central nervous system but seem to be due to the direct action of the drug on the smooth muscle.[12] It was formerly held that morphine was the direct cause of tissue deterioration, but we now know that a decrease in appetite brings about the shocking malnutrition so commonly seen in addicts. They simply do not take in sufficient calories to maintain normal weight. Opium's action on the smooth muscle is one of contraction, which explains its use for relieving diarrhea. Besides diminishing gastric motility, it causes a contraction of the pyloric sphincter, thus slowing down the digestive process at an early stage.

In the small intestine, morphine produces an increase in the muscular tone, further delaying the propulsion of food and thus allowing more of the fluid content to be absorbed.

The large intestine is likely to be most affected by morphine. In fact its tone may be increased to the extent that repeated spasms occur. X-ray may reveal the complete absence of peristalsis.

Pupils

Constriction of the pupils, always considered an unwavering symptom of morphinism, is clinically unreliable. The pupils may acquire a kind of tolerance for morphine and thus not show the marked constriction produced by a single dose or even the degree observed in the early stages of addiction.

It is now known that pupillary constriction is a result of stimulation rather than retardation of the parasympathetic nerves. If the pupil is locally dilated with a sympathomimetic drug it will fail to constrict when its sympathetic chain is blocked, but when morphine is administered the dilated pupil will constrict.

Blood Vessels

An exception to its usual contracting action on smooth muscle is found in morphine's effect on the peripheral vascular system. The blood vessels not only fail to constrict peripherally but they may in fact dilate—as evidenced by the frequency of fainting and dizziness among morphine users.

Heart

There is no evidence that morphine acts directly on the cardiac muscle; any seeming cardiac effects are due to a large amount of the morphine acting on a central vasomotor depression center.

Morphine's possible effect on the electrocardiogram—an abnormal alteration of the T waves—may be due to the relative anoxia of the myocardium, due to the concomitant respiratory depression. This should be borne in mind in cases of acute coronary thrombosis, when morphine is routinely administered.

Shock-like Reactions

A single dose of morphine may also have effects resembling the shock which follows minor surgery or accidents—

sweating and a drop in the systolic and diastolic pressure with an initial tachycardia. There may be itching and flushing of the skin. These reactions may give way to bradycardia, a drop in body temperature and a decreased respiration rate with retention of water throughout the body.

Central Nervous System

Site of Action. Not all functions of the central nervous system are subject to morphine's depressant effect; for instance, the sense of hearing and the sense of smell are exceptions. However, its action is not limited to one region of the brain but seems to range from the cortex to the diencephalon, pons, thalamus, medulla, and thence to the spinal cord and the vegetative nervous system. The motor cortex is usually involved only when massive doses of morphine have been administered. Until recently it was thought that morphine's site of action was the medullary centers exclusively, but further research has revealed that it may work directly on the vago reflex centers in the pons to produce the characteristic depressed respiration and vomiting.

Subjective Equivalents. Morphine's early appellation, "God's medicine," referred to its pain-relieving qualities. Now we see that in addition to its pain-killing properties two basic bodily drives of mankind are satisfied by morphine: hunger and sex. The action on the central nervous system is such that the user feels he has eaten to his heart's content, experienced full sexual satisfaction, and eliminated all his anxieties as well. One begins to see that the behavior of addicts is bound to be utterly different from that of people whose major drive centers around appeasing these basic life factors.

Pain. In trying to discover just how morphine affects pain, physiologists find themselves at a crossroad in human behavior where an individual's past emotional experiences fuse with his present organic stimulation.

Although the exact site in the brain of morphine's action on pain is not known, its effect on anxiety resembles that of a prefrontal lobotomy. This resemblance strongly suggests the frontal lobes as the site of much of morphine's pain-killing action.

The imminence of pain produces in human beings a condition known as anticipatory anxiety, filling them with fears and mobilizing them for flight. Such people may perceive a sudden pin prick as a stab. It has been shown that when this side reaction of pain—anticipatory anxiety—is eliminated, morphine acts to raise the pain threshold. Research on morphine and pain has made us broaden our definition of pain experiences, which are found to be "composed not only of pain sensation but of associated sensations and of emotional and affective states as well."[15] As can be seen, this definition covers those patients whose pain (real or imaginary) diminishes following reassurance, re-education or placebos.

Hardy, Wolff and Goodell[15] in their work on the pain-threshold-raising action of morphine discovered that *suggestion* could modify analgesic effects. The majority of subjects who were given a narcotic, meperidine, but told that it might be a placebo either had no effects or a *lowered* pain threshold. Conversely, subjects who were given to believe that the shot was an analgesic but were instead given placebos demonstrated a measurable increase in their pain threshold.

Those who are skeptical of these findings on the grounds that the pain was artificially induced may find corroboration of this experiment in an article by Beecher.[16] He found that approximately one-third of a large group of patients who had had major surgery were completely relieved of their pain through suggestion and subcutaneous injections of a saline placebo.

Of the eight modes of action of analgesics listed by Hardy and his co-workers,[15] the opiates were found to raise the pain threshold by "reducing pain, suppression of reflexes, and alteration in attitude."

Here, too, mention should be made of the analgesic effect of barbiturates. It was found by Hardy et al.[15] that barbiturates have little analgesic action unless the subject is allowed to sleep. As sleep is considered to be an analgesic factor, any raising of the pain threshold by barbiturates is actually indirect, due intrinsically to the sleep.

Electroencephalography. Although research at Lexington includes considerable encephalographic study of humans and animals, there is a long way to go before evidence can be said to be conclusive. When animals are given morphine in sufficient dosages to produce convulsions, the E.E.G. exhibits spike and dome patterns. These patterns seem to point to an involvement of the motor cortex and possibly the medial nucleus of the thalamus. According to Andrews' study,[13] the E.E.G.'s of drug addicts reveal a higher alpha percentage than those of normal non-addicted people. Dr. Wikler found that after dogs were injected with morphine their E.E.G. changes were similar to those observed in humans during deep sleep.[14] Further research suggests that the E.E.G. changes may be attributed to a depression of the reticular activating mechanism in the diencephalon and mid-brain.

TOLERANCE

The phenomenon of tolerance—a diminution in the effectiveness of a drug with repeated use—occurs in addiction to opium and its derivatives as well as to barbiturates. Despite the many theories advanced to explain the phenomenon of tolerance, it is not yet clearly understood. However, certain recent research studies show, as has been stated, that metabolic dysfunction is a factor.

Addicts may build up an enormous tolerance to morphine; in experimental studies as high as 75 grains a day have been administered. A wryly humorous incident occurred during an experiment at Lexington. When an addict had reached a very high tolerance level, he complained of an earache and insisted on being given Sulfadiazine, which he was sure would relieve it!

Tolerance can be built up very rapidly. Experiments in which a patient was allowed to receive any drug he wished, at any time, in any form, and in the desired amount, demonstrated that a tolerance to approximately 1200 milligrams a day could be built up in four months' time.[17] Even with a steady use of the drug over a long period an individual does not build up a tolerance to all the effects of morphine; that is to say, tolerance never becomes absolute. No matter how high a drug addict's tolerance, he can still administer a lethal dose to himself, even though he can handle a single shot eight times the strength of his usual dosage. With repeated use, morphine ceases to have a depressant effect on respiration. Constipation may give way to diarrhea. There may be no perceptible constriction of the pupils. Some of the psychological effects of well-being are likely to diminish and the cardiac rate may return to normal.

Many pharmacologists have assumed the phenomenon of tolerance and withdrawal symptoms were intimately connected. But since the advent of the new drug N-allylnormorphine (Nalline-Merck) this assumption has been challenged, and new areas of research along the lines of the Dual Action theory have been opened.

N-allylnormorphine (see further discussion in Chapter II, page 27) is a drug which has the property of reversing the action of morphine. It artificially produces withdrawal symptoms in drug addicts—identical with the symptoms which follow the withholding of morphine from an addict. The one notable difference, which gives credence to the Dual Action theory, is that the "artificial" withdrawal symptoms *cannot be relieved by administering morphine*. In fact, there seems to be a refractory period during which morphine does not counteract the effects of the new drug. This suggests that withdrawal symptoms are not connected with the phenomenon of tolerance but are indeed the result of the unmasked excitatory factor of morphine.

Clinically speaking, the depressant effects of morphine gradually recede, but the excitatory effects continue. Euphoria and/or the orgastic type of reaction is experienced with each succeeding shot only if the dosage is increased. If the dosage remains the same, the patient's tolerance may cause him to experience slight withdrawal symptoms.

It has been generally believed that a patient does not acquire a tolerance to morphine short of repeated administration for many weeks. But research with N-allylnormorphine has shown that withdrawal symptoms can be precipitated in animals after as few as eight doses of morphine within a period of two days[3]; and in humans, tolerance has been demonstrated after morphine has been administered for one week.[4]

This study proves that tolerance to morphine develops before it can be observed clinically. Although research on this new drug is not complete, it appears to be in line for many uses both in the office diagnosis and in hospital procedures, to detect subclinical addiction.

Addicts dislike the problems attending addiction and tolerance; and for this reason they continually enter hospitals voluntarily to have their habit reduced. Some others try to confine themselves to occasional shots spaced far enough apart so that they will not build up a tolerance of any kind. This is the same kind of losing battle fought by the alcoholic who tries to limit his drinking to an occasional cocktail or highball.

ABSTINENCE SYNDROME

The abstinence syndrome resulting from the withholding of morphine demonstrates that physical dependency on the drug is one of the major characteristics of opiate addiction. Although recognized by the medical profession, these withdrawal symptoms as recently as 1920 were generally believed to be largely hysterical in origin. Research at Lexington was directed toward determining whether withdrawal symptoms had an organic base or constituted primarily a psychological problem. It was found that the physical responses occurring in animals and in humans are identical. It therefore seems reasonable to assume that addiction and withdrawal symptoms occur on a level of integration that does not require bringing the higher mental centers into play.

Dogs were used in further exploratory studies to determine what parts of the brain must remain intact for withdrawal symptoms to occur. The animals were prepared by completely removing the neo-cortex and were then addicted to morphine. When the morphine was withheld, the observed symptoms were vomiting, tearing, salivation, etc., just as in intact humans.[5]

These experiments prove beyond doubt that withdrawal symptoms are specifically of sub-cortical origin.

An unusual case of a man addicted to drugs who was subjected to a bilateral frontal lobotomy is reported in the literature. When the drugs were stopped after surgery, he showed withdrawal symptoms.[6] This rare case parallels in a human the responses of the decorticate dogs.

It has been shown that morphine addiction involves the spinal cord neurons. Animals were prepared by sectioning the spinal cord at the level of cervical six and seven. After addiction and abrupt withdrawal of morphine, these spinal animals demonstrated hyperactive flexor and crossed extensor reflexes followed by spontaneous running movements in the hind limbs.[7] The fact that withdrawal symptoms appear in animals with a severed spinal cord suggests that the tremors and twitchings in human addicts are due to a hyperexcitability of the internuncial neurons of the spinal cord.

The abstinence syndrome is broken down, for clinical and research purposes, into two large categories: (1) the purposive signs, (2) the non-purposive signs.

The purposive signs relate to the patient's subjective feelings and behavior during withdrawal which are centered around obtaining more drugs. The non-purposive signs include clinical evidences such as lacrimation, rhinorrhea, yawning, sweating, reduced eosinophile count, elevated temperature and blood pressure, vomiting, and diarrhea—described in varying degrees of intensity, so that clinicians refer to mild, moderate or severe withdrawal symptoms (see Chapter VI).

The purposive signs were formerly believed to be evidence of the drug addict's shrewdness. However, their presence in the lower primates used in research suggests that this so-called shrewdness is itself a part of the total abstinence syndrome.

The abstinence syndrome sets in about twelve hours after the last administration of the drug. Its intensity depends principally on the size of the addict's habit. Mild symptoms give way to moderately severe symptoms within twenty-four hours: the pupils dilate widely, goose flesh appears and the muscles begin to twitch uncontrollably. If untreated, the patient's symptoms reach a peak somewhere between the forty-eighth and the seventy-second hour after his last shot. On the third day of withdrawal the signs of physical dependency subside and the patient is left physically and emotionally depleted.

RELAPSE

The phenomenon of relapse, inherent in our over-all definition, is the least understood mechanism in addiction. It has been considered sufficient to explain it on the basis of psychological and social factors. There is no doubt that drug addicts find it easier to resume their known way of life than to face the certain anxieties and the uncertain pleasures of carving out a new life.

It is no wonder that the general public is badly confused about the relative importance of relapse in the total picture of drug addiction. On the one hand, medical authorities in the field write that "only a small percentage of addicts have no desire either to get off drugs or to remain off,"[18] whereas other medical authorities have estimated relapse rates as high as 95 per cent. The facts are that, with rare exceptions, all addicts would like to go off drugs and stay off, but few of them are convinced that they could do so. There is no question that relapse, an ever-present possibility, is one of the factors making the treatment of addiction so difficult. The problems of relapse have not been sufficiently explored largely because there are not enough patients under medical treatment, nor do we have much solid information about ex-addicts. Lexington has supplied considerable data on active addicts and their recidivistic problems.

There may also be a pharmacogenic factor in relapse. It is quite common for addicts, during a period of imprisonment when they are entirely off drugs, to report subjectively experienced withdrawal symptoms. Their descriptions are bolstered by many observable withdrawal signs—dilated pupils, sweating, pallor, lacrimation, etc.—during this period of intense craving for drugs. Whether they are unconsciously reproducing the signs of physical dependence, or whatever the cause, there is no doubt that the central nervous system is involved; and the accompanying symptoms virtually force the patient to try to obtain drugs for relief.

Conclusive research on addiction is hampered by the paucity of our knowledge of the physiology of man's basic drives: hunger, sexuality and self-preservation. Research dealing with the physiology of grief, rage and anxiety is still in its infancy, despite the fact that physicians must cope with these emotions or problems resulting from them in their daily practice. Perhaps in time this vast reservoir will be tapped.

Conclusions from the research in addiction seem to lead with similar precision to ever-widening meanings in different areas of human behavior. One begins to wonder about man's personal and historical struggle to avoid pain; and to compare his relentless struggle to achieve security in society with the addict's similar struggle to obtain drugs which produce in him the same desired feeling of security. Perhaps the obsessional drive in both instances is the same. Surely the work drive of the scientist or businessman, which may exclude even his family and friends, is similar though more "normal" than the drive of the addict pursuing his drugs.

Indeed, it seems reasonable to suppose that the accumulation of more complete data on the subject of drug addiction will contribute a share toward unraveling the mystery behind human behavior. Such holistic thinking can lead to premature conclusions which may be manifestly absurd. However, with this limitation in mind, it can also lead to further experimentation which may prove rewarding.

REFERENCES

1. Pierce, I. H., and Blant, O. H.: Studies of chronic morphine poisoning in dogs. IV. Excretion of morphine in tolerant and non-tolerant animals. J. Pharmacol. & Exper. Therap. 46: 201-228, 1932.
2. Oberst, F. W.: Free and bound morphine in the urine of morphine addicts. J. Pharmacol. & Exper. Therap. 69: 240-251, 1940.
3. Wikler, A. and Carter, R. L.: Effects of morphine and N-allylnormorphine on reflexes in dog and cat. Fed. Proc. 11: 402, 1952.
4. Wikler, A. et. al.: Precipitation of "abstinence syndromes" by single doses of N-allylnormorphine in addicts. Fed. Proc. 11: 402, 1952.

5. Wikler, A.: Reactions of dogs without neo-cortex during cycles of addiction to morphine and methadone. Arch. Neurol. & Psychiat. *67:* 672-684, 1952.

6. Wikler, A., Pescor, M. J., Kalbaugh, E. M., and Angelucci, R. J.: The effects of frontal lobotomy on the morphine abstinence syndrome in man. Arch. Neurol. & Psychiat. *67:* 510-521, 1952.

7. Wikler, A. and Frank, K.: Hindlimb reflexes of chronic spinal dogs during cycles of addiction to morphine and methadone. J. Pharmacol. & Exper. Therap. *94:* 382, 1948.

8. Wikler, A., and Rayport, M.: Lower limb reflexes during a cycle of morphine addiction in a chronic "spinal" man. (In preparation.)

9. Tatum, A. L., Seevers, M. H., and Collins, K. H.: Morphine addiction and its physiological interpretation based on experimental evidences. J. Pharmacol. & Exper. Therap. *36:* 447-475, 1929.

10. Spragg, S. D. S.: Morphine addiction in chimpanzees. Comp. Psychol. Monogr. *15:* 1-132, 1940.

11. McCarthy, W.: A prosecutor's viewpoint on narcotic addiction. Federal Probation *1:* 23-27, 1943.

12. Krueger, A.: Action of morphine on the digestive tract. Physiol. Rev. *17:* 618, 1937.

13. Andrews, H. L.: Brain potentials and morphine addiction. Psychosom. Med. *3:* 399, 1941.

14. Wikler, A.: Drug addiction. In Tice's Practice of Medicine, vol. 8. Hagerstown, Prior, 1953.

15. Hardy, J. D., Wolff, H. G., and Goodell, B. S.: Pain Sensations and Reactions. Baltimore, William and Wilkins, 1952.

16. Beecher, H K.: Pain in men wounded in battle. Bull. U. S. Army Med. Dept. *5:* 445 1946.

17. Wikler, A.: A psychodynamic study of a patient during experimental self-regulated re-addiction to morphine. Psychiat. Quart. *26:* 270-293, 1952.

18. Maurer, D. W., and Vogel, V. H.: Narcotics and Narcotic Addiction. Springfield C. C Thomas, 1954. P. 163.

IV. Psychology

THE QUESTION OF what drives a person to become a drug addict has always aroused the curiosity of the non-addict world. Because normal people can scarcely imagine what forces could impel others into the maelstrom of subjective experience described by drug addicts, such books as DeQuincey's *Confessions of an English Opium Eater* (1821) have found a large and eager audience. Apart from the attraction of the off-beat and the forbidden, there seems to be a natural inclination for man to try to understand his fellow creatures, no matter what ills have befallen them.

So difficult is it to understand—to say nothing of trying to befriend—drug addicts, that, as we have seen, there is great hostility toward them as a group. Many who start out with a sincere interest have wound up with a bitter judgmental attitude. Workers in this field have consistently found that the tremendous suffering of the drug addict evokes little sympathy in people who normally respond to suffering of any kind. This great gap is in turn sensed by the drug addict: to know that he suffers is one thing, but to feel his suffering or care about it is quite another.

The addict is a self-made outcast. Whatever are his problems, his inept attempts to solve them take him into another world where only his fellow addicts can appreciate them, and this withdrawal further barricades him from "outside" help. As we shall see, this lack of humanity for the drug addict is a valid reaction, but not the less unfortunate because it is of his own making. It is in the nature of the drug addict's problem not to seek or avail himself of help.

Is drug addiction an illness or a symptom? In other words, is addiction determined by the chemical action of the drug or by the psychological structure of the individual? As we shall see later in this text, the pharmacological effects of morphine on the central nervous system are not influenced by race, reli-

57

gion, social stratum or occupation. It would thus appear to be true that the drug itself determines addiction, from which no one is immune, leaving little room in the picture for personality determinants.

However, this explanation does not cover all observable facts. As Lindesmith in his book, *Opiate Addiction*,[16] points out, there are still many questions that need to be answered. How can we explain the fact that of two people exposed to drugs one will repeat the experiment again and again until addiction is produced, whereas the other will show no further interest? The first introduction to a drug, nine times out of ten, takes place in a social situation in which the person incidentally hears about drugs, sees them used or is directly told about them. Thus a social factor must of necessity play a part. It would then follow that the potential addict's response to the social situation must differ from that of the non-addict, throwing a focus upon the personality structure even before the first shot is taken.

Dr. Lindesmith reports on the experiences of several physicians in Germany, where opiates are used in treating severe manic-depressive psychosis and melancholia. Strangely enough, out of the hundreds of patients under their care, no psychotic patient became addicted despite the repeated use of opiates. Similarly, he cites articles in the literature reporting cases of children who became medically addicted before the age of ten. In almost none of these cases was addiction a problem in the child's later life. It would therefore seem that there are factors other than the purely pharmacological ones which determine who will become addicted and who will not.

This conclusion brings us logically to a study of the pre-addiction personality and the changes noticeable after addiction is established. Just as the medical person uses x-ray and laboratory tests in making a physical diagnosis, so are there similar routines to determine the personality structure. For a psychological diagnosis the psychiatrist depends on the results of a careful work-up called the mental status, psychological tests such as the Rorschach, and the patient's responses as revealed by the technique of psychoanalysis. We shall here attempt to examine the psychological findings of the drug addict's make-up and give the current explanation for these findings.

THE ADDICT'S PERSONALITY

Mental Status during Addiction

The mental status examination, used for testing the various capacities of the brain, will uncover alterations in cerebral functioning whether of emotional or organic origin. The psychiatrist thus covers some of the same ground which falls within the province of the neurologist.

Unless he is under the influence of his drug or in a state of severe lack of it or other physical distress, the addict's appearance is not likely to be unusual (although there may be an appearance of illness, as we shall see in Chapter VI). He has no definite mannerisms, tics, postures, motor disturbances or dysarthria. His gait is normal; his speech unimpaired, with no evidence of slurring; in short, there are no clean-cut and invariable manifestations of his illness (see Chapter VI).

The addict's behavior during his first interview with the physician will very probably show no marked abnormalities. His manner is usually serious; he answers questions relevantly and behaves in general according to the demands of the situation.

The drug addict's emotional reactions associated with his experiences, however, appear to be somewhat blunted; that is, he does not seem to be suffering the degree of nervousness or emotional tension warranted by the experiences he is relating. While he is describing his manifold difficulties such as the recent loss of his wife and children because of his addiction, one does not have the feeling that he is actually deeply concerned or holding back tears. There is a general flatness in his delivery. Although he may laugh at what would to a normal person be a harrowing experience, one does not perceive this as the inappropriate affect of the schizophrenic. It seems rather to have a certain logic predicated upon his own personal needs at the time.

The major part of the drug addict's conversation centers around his own problems with addiction and obtaining drugs.

60 THE DRUG ADDICT AS A PATIENT

He seldom talks about his possible effect on others but is entirely absorbed with himself and his rationalizations to stay on drugs or go off drugs. These rationalizations are again based entirely upon his own experiences and his motivation seldom includes the welfare of others.

The sensorium of a drug addict is always clear, unless he is also taking alcohol or barbiturates, when there may be evidence of disorientation with reference to time or place or people. Both his recent and his past memory are unchanged; his judgment and sense of right and wrong are impaired only when turned inward on his own life's course. Retention and recall, simple mathematics, conceptual thinking are all intact and there is no evidence of mental deterioration.[1, 2] If there is any clouding of the sensorium, one must suspect some organic difficulty if neither alcohol nor another drug plays a part.

The large scale intelligence testing of addicts in prisons and public hospitals shows their IQ rating to be close to that of the general population.[3] Although several studies have come up with a figure slightly below average, tests of addicts in private hospitals revealed an IQ of 113, which is above the national average.[4] Intelligence tests of addicts while on and off drugs show no appreciable difference[3] nor do tests of their capacity for physical performance, no matter how many years they have been on drugs—a rather astonishing fact in view of their completely unproductive lives. Incidentally, there are apparently no organic changes in the central nervous system that would prevent an addict from living a productive life even while on drugs.

Rorschach Studies

The Rorschach (ink blot) test is a valuable and reliable aid in personality evaluation. The various amorphous shapes and forms evoke various responses which in turn have been carefully studied and statistically grouped. The so-called popular responses, anxiety responses, etc., when analyzed correspond to the clinical findings of psychiatrists. This fact further reinforces the validity and importance of Rorschach findings in uncovering a patient's deeper drives and personality structure.

Rorschach studies at Lexington[15] indicate a marked constriction of the average patient's personality and confirm his already apparent immaturity. With the administration of morphine a striking change is observed in the Rorschach—a change which corresponds to the addict's subjective feeling that he has attained normalcy. The responses begin to fall into more normal categories; the constriction is lessened, and movement response and fantasy appear.

But these results, however significant, constitute only meager evidence that morphine brings about personality changes. Conclusive proof must rest on whether or not the constriction found in the addict's tests was present *before* he became addicted. If not, it may safely be assumed to be the result of social and emotional regression.

Moral Judgment

There is a peculiar dichotomy in the addict's moral judgment. The addict who is not ashamed of his own addiction is a distinct rarity. And he is also deeply concerned about causing someone else to become addicted, vowing that he "wouldn't wish this thing on his worst enemy." But, curiously enough, when the subject of peddlers who introduce adolescents to drugs is brought up, or the truly heartrending trials endured by the families of addicts, there is an almost total lack of sympathetic response. At this point the addict sees the drug peddler as his benefactor, the alleviator of his distress, and the magnitude of this act makes it impossible for him to be objective about the peddler's role in enslaving others. Similarly, the addict's own distress is to him the only meaningful distress: "Nobody else can suffer as much as I do, so why should I worry about them?" Neither in conversation nor in therapy can one appeal to an addict by pointing out any of the consequences to his family. The motivation generally comes right back to himself.

This blind spot in moral judgment is quite understandable from the addict's viewpoint; he cannot be expected to turn on those who constantly supply relief for his withdrawal suffering. With the exception of this area, the addict shows great moral indignation at outrages committed in society and is inclined to be very self-righteous in his manner. One cannot help seeing that his moral judgments and his repugnance for the barbarous actions of alcoholics, sexual degenerates, murderers and the like, are in no small degree a defense of his own comparatively innocuous social behavior.

Psychiatric Diagnosis

Personality classifications have been made on large groups of addicts. Examination of the data from psychiatric studies indicates that the milieu in which the addict is studied is an index to the diagnosis. Among the addicts studied at Lexington and in city and state prisons there is a preponderance of psychopaths,[5] whereas they make up only a small percentage of the patients examined in private institutions.

The incidence of insanity among addicts is the same as in the general population. Although the great majority have no history of mental disorders, only a few could be classified as normal, well-adjusted people. People who become medically addicted in the course of a serious illness, as well as Orientals brought up in a culture where the smoking of opium is socially accepted, fall into a group who might be said to approach normalcy while sustaining their addiction. But the majority of patients come under the classification of constitutional psychopathic inferior, character disorder or psychoneurosis.

Some workers in the field of drug addiction believe that all addicts might well be classified as sub-clinical schizophrenics. Their severe obsessional preoccupation with drugs and the destructiveness of their pursuits in an otherwise normal personality are so bizarre as to be strongly suggestive of schizophrenia. In support of this theory, it may be pointed out that patients whose behavior is so negligibly guided by reality reveal the disordered thinking characteristic of that condition. This is further confirmed by observation in a number of post-addicts of psychosis which disappears with the administration of morphine.

The diagnosis of psychopathic personality is based on actual anti-social or criminal activities. To what extent a drug

addict's criminal behavior results from his addiction rather
than from any abnormal personality defects is still debated.
Reports of the United States Bureau of Narcotics[6] seem to
indicate criminal activity in the majority of drug addicts before the onset of their addiction. Conversely, random studies
made at Lexington reveal that in the majority of cases there
was no criminal activity antedating addiction. It would seem
reasonable to conclude that criminals living on the fringes of
society may become addicted through association with underworld figures who control the illegal drug traffic. These addicts
would therefore have the true psychopathic personality, rather
than those whose anti-social behavior is not an intrinsic personality defect but grows out of circumventing existing laws.

One of the remarkable gaps in the sociological studies is
the lack of evidence of any control groups. For instance, to my
knowledge there has never been a study to determine whether
the degree of psychopathic behavior in drug addicts is any
greater than that found in a non-addict group of comparable
economic, social and educational level. Zimmering[7] in his personality study of twenty-two adolescent boy drug addicts hospitalized at Bellevue describes them as non-aggressive, soft-
spoken and verbally apt. He notes that these boys were unable
to develop genuine human relationships. They appeared generally immature, easily moved to extreme emotional reactions,
and unable to tolerate frustration. A constriction of emotional
reactions and marked feelings of inferiority were present in
all of them. Observing them on the ward, he found that they
reacted to the frustrations which inevitably occur in daily living by withdrawal or by dependency.

There seems to be a unanimity of opinion concerning the
personality of drug addicts: they are markedly immature and
withdrawn and have an overwhelming feeling of inadequacy.
They have no confidence in their ability to do anything on
their own and hence must rely on others to help them obtain
what they want. This description of the character structure of
the drug addict is all right as far as it goes but it doesn't go
far enough, for the characteristics agreed on for the drug addict are not significantly different from those found within

the general non-addict population. Here we come up against a factor of paramount importance; if there is no significant difference between the personality structure of addicts and non-addicts, drug addiction would seem to be due primarily to the action of drugs, and its incidence in the population would depend on chance experiencing of the effect of drugs. If, on the other hand, it can be shown that the potential addict has a specific combination of psychological factors which produce an impulse that can be handled *only* by the administration of drugs, these psychological factors will then become truly meaningful.

THEORETICAL FORMULATIONS

Theory of Avoidance of Sex

One of the significant facts drawn from a general examination of the drug addict's total life span is that the habit frequently begins in adolescence or in the early twenties, is maintained through the next two decades and dwindles out in the mid forties. This same time span is observed to cover with some regularity alcoholism, delinquency and criminality. That these twenty-five to thirty years are normally the most active of one's lifetime, is a coincidence arousing considerable speculation. What happens to drug addicts to bring about this change in the forties? Have they finally decided that the few months of pleasure which they enjoy on drugs are hardly worth the many years in prison that result? Have they, with advancing age, lost the necessary energy and guile to stay outside of the law? Or, if one considers that their anti-social behavior is rooted in great hostility toward authorities and defiance of their laws, could it be that this hostility has been spent through the years?

These are no doubt some of the possible factors in the larger emotional problems created by drug addiction. However, in addition, one cannot overlook the fact that the addiction period covers man's most active sexual years. Adolescence as we know is characterized by the awakening of sexual feelings and aggressions. With the passing of adolescence the individual's sexual yearnings have in most cases been gratified. Is there a correlation between an adolescent's experiencing of the yearnings accompanying his own developing sexuality and his attempts to find gratifications by means other than the normal maturation of this phase of his life?

Our attention is further focused upon the possibility of the adolescent's fear of sexuality, when we consider that narcotics are known to diminish sexual activity to the zero point. We know from the action of morphine on the central nervous system that the addict feels as satisfied in this regard as if he had already performed coitus. In this light the adolescent addict's search for his next shot appears to be an activity which supplants looking for a "hot" date. On questioning, he may relate that his few attempts at sexual relationships have been attended with considerable fear and relatively little satisfaction. Furthermore, it has been established that mixed groups of addicts do not indulge in any form of sexuality.

Looking at the far side of the addiction span, the parallel still holds true, for the addict usually gives up drugs at the time of life when sexuality begins to diminish. In effect, he manages to live his life in such a way as to avoid the normal gratification of sexual longings experienced by others.

Whether this avoidance of sexuality is a cause or a result of addiction is open to question. But regardless of this aspect, the addict's life does not include what could by any stretch of the imagination be called normal sexuality.

Avoidance of Aggression Theory

The span from adolescence to middle age, which includes man's active sexual life, also marks his active assuming of responsibility, his mobilization of sufficient security and aggression to enable him satisfactorily to perform the functions of a mature adult. The addict rarely develops any skill or trade which would enable him to provide for himself, to say nothing of a potential family. With the exception of physicians and nurses, drug addicts are by and large a singularly unskilled group (see Chapter V, page 89).

Psychiatric interviews corroborate the manifestations of the inner feelings of drug addicts. Once their thin layer of bravado is gone, their profound feelings of inadequacy are revealed—the complete lack of self-confidence in their ability to compete successfully with other men in society. Their responses have an interesting and revealing sequence. After they have discussed their feelings of inadequacy to cope with the outside world, they invariably quickly turn to their successes in the drug addict world: the important people they know, their ability to obtain drugs at any time, and their wide connections with peddlers. It is as if their self-importance in the world of drug addicts must be built up to counterbalance their failure in the outside world.

Immature personality, the psychiatric classification of those individuals who have developed little ability either to meet their own needs or those of a family, fits the average addict perfectly. With almost no means of obtaining satisfaction from any kind of constructive aggression, he rationalizes his fate as a complete indifference to the conventional values. But on carefully penetrating his indifference and apathy, to ascertain his feelings before drug addiction became a complicating and all-absorbing problem in his life, one finds that he harbored a deep fear that he could not make his way in the world and provide a living as other men do.

It is typical of drug addicts to lack the same psychological drive, pleasures and goals which begin to emerge in normal adolescents and are crystallized in the normal mature adult. The psychiatrist's goal is to find out why the addict does not follow this normal pattern, and what are the drives, pleasures and goals of the pattern he does follow. At what point does the addict's illness set in? Does the fact of addiction in an adolescent or young adult mark the beginning of his illness, or did it actually begin with a psychiatric problem which predisposed him to turn to addiction at this particular time?

The Wikler Theory

The theoretical formulations of Dr. Abraham Wikler of Lexington Hospital are of such vital importance as to warrant special and detailed attention. Dr. Wikler has the unique advantage of advanced psychiatric training as well as outstanding ability in the field of neurophysiology. His conceptual theories, based on original research with animal and human subjects, are at once the most comprehensive and inclusive that we have to date.

In his paper on the psychiatric aspects of drug addiction,[12] Wikler reviews his observations of patients actively addicted under experimental conditions. He is impressed with the fact that antisocial behavior and aggression are seldom observed; in fact, patients on drugs discharge their responsibilities satisfactorily and show little if any psychological impairment. By contrast, addicts under the influence of barbiturates or alcohol become hostile, and undergo an appreciable dulling of the sensorium.

Because different groups of drugs alter behavior in different ways, he concludes that its specific desirable effect leads the individual to choose a certain drug. The alcoholic who becomes openly aggressive chooses alcohol in order to release his pent-up emotions. Such a person would in all probability be found to have an idealized image of himself as a tough character. Similarly, the drug addict, who desires in his inmost self to be quiet, untroubled and contemplative, chooses the drug which will facilitate such an effect. Alcohol reduces inhibitions, with the result that some alcoholics characteristically become belligerent, exhibitionistic, licentious, irresponsible, and so on. A humorous saying popular among addicts—the alcoholic gets drunk, goes home and beats up his wife, but old dopey takes a shot, goes home and his wife beats him up—has some basis in fact. Dr. Kolb,[13] in a discussion of addicts in relation to crime, mentions the power of opium to reduce vicious criminal tendencies. Criminals with a history of violence lost all such violent activity as part of their behavior pattern after becoming addicted. The user's choice of drug reveals what makes him feel at his best, and in general the drug addict is most comfortable when his hostility and aggression are blunted, as with opiates.

In an unusual experiment,[14] Wikler was able to study, both psychiatrically and organically, a post-addict who, under the conditions of the experiment, was allowed to avail himself of all the drugs he wanted at any time in any amount. He was told that he would be given one month's notice before the drugs were discontinued. The patient was seen several times a week for psychiatric interviews before, during and after the experiment.

It is most interesting to learn that, although the patient was in prison and taking part in an experiment, he experienced guilt, which under the conditions can be interpreted only as resulting from his pleasure in the use of the drugs per se. Since the drugs were legally dispensed he would, of course, not suffer any untoward consequences from his indulgence and in theory he should have been able to enjoy himself to the fullest, under the unique terms of the experiment. Instead, in the beginning the patient resolved not to become addicted. His guilt about breaking this resolution was reflected in the fact that he was ashamed to explain to the rabbi why he had not attended religious services. But his guilt was swiftly shelved as the patient succumbed to the large doses of morphine he administered to himself.

As the experiment drew to a close the patient was given notice that in one month all drugs would be abruptly discontinued. He began systematically to reduce his dosage and continued quite successfully up till the last few days of the month, when he undid all his careful reduction work in one fell swoop and upped his dosage quickly to fifteen grains a day. By the final date he was caught with an extremely strong habit and could anticipate a very rough withdrawal period. Wikler suggests that the almost planned painful withdrawal may be a way in which the drug addict expiated his guilt; a negation of his pleasure from the drug. This may also explain why addicts in interviews show so little guilt. They may consider the countless times they have suffered a withdrawal period to be sufficient atonement for the current anti-social or narcissistic pursuit of their habit.

Careful interrogation of this patient led Wikler to believe that terms such as "feeling normal," commonly used by addicts to describe the effect of drugs, really means to them a gratification of primary needs: hunger and sexual urges, and removal of the fear of pain. It would seem that as addiction progresses, tolerance itself develops into a force, assuming the same character and magnitude as hunger and sexual urges, thus becoming a primary need that can be satisfied only with a morphine-like drug.

Wikler concludes that "former narcotic addicts, regardless of conventional personality classifications which may be applied to them, are individuals in whom the chief sources of anxiety are related to pain, sexuality and the expression of aggression." His theory is in accord with the fact that addiction frequently begins in adolescence, a period characterized by awakened sexuality and the necessity to assume an aggressive role in society. He makes a special point of noting that morphine's instantaneous alleviation of the abstinence syndrome cannot help making the relieved person place great value on the drug.

ATTITUDES TOWARD SELF

Self-Preoccupation and Self-Destruction

We have seen that the addict avoids situations involving mature sexuality, social responsibility and worldly competitiveness. His world is actually made up of himself and his problems. His manifest behavior does not include any activity which involves giving to any loved one, friend or family member, or even to society. Such a total lack of giving is very rare and is found in very few emotional disorders. Many a spinster who sorely misses the joys of a family of her own gives to others a great deal of thoughtful consideration and love, perhaps as a teacher or nurse, and regardless of the reason for the bachelor's avoidance of the responsibility of his own family, he meets the responsibilities of a daily job and does not shun social contacts.

The drug addict's self-destructive bent is apparent even to casual observers. Nothing in his entire picture can be considered constructive from his personal viewpoint. The continuance of his illness destroys any possibility for achieving, much less keeping, those rights which all men expect to make their own: the rights of freedom, happiness, friendship, work, security and health. At every turn he jeopardizes these rights. Given the opportunity either to gratify an immediate impulse or to gain a long term satisfaction, the addict invariably chooses the former.

That his illness has an essential core of self-destructiveness is well known to the drug addict but rarely acknowledged by him. He avoids facing up to it by immersing himself in the daily struggle to obtain drugs, which in turn give him temporary gratification, and he completes the circle by denying the over-all self-destructiveness of his illness.

Any person's self-destructive impulses may cause unpleasant incidents in his life, but the drug addict's self-destructiveness is so complete and thoroughly shattering that there seems to be no way back for him. His relationships with family and friends have perhaps been irreparably spoiled. He has usually proved so unreliable on any job that he cannot get adequate references if he should want to work. If he has been in prison, either his inability to account for those years or his fingerprints may give him away, making his employment very improbable. Thus he creates a realistic situation which puts him out of the running, so to speak. His fears about himself become facts and construct a further barrier to normal rehabilitation.

One who has had long experience with drug addicts recognizes that they derive a considerable amount of pleasure from their self-destruction. Their eagerness, after an absence, to plunge immediately back into the familiar struggles of the addict and to sense the excitement of procuring drugs on the black market, is a typical manifestation of their masochism.

Narcissism

In general, the only aggressive and purposeful pattern followed by the addict is his pursuit of drugs for self-administration. His thoughts, actions and associations with others are usually meaningless unless they help toward this goal. The addict quickly drops any people who are of no use to him, and thus his personal relationships are soon confined to the drug world. He has no time, energy or thought to expend on people in any interchange; he neither gives of himself nor has pleasure in satisfying another, as a love partner. We see him ever in search of his own gratification and never in the aggressive act of giving. This type of individual whose entire life is absorbed in self-gratifications is known as a narcissist. Every normal personality has a small component of narcissism and it is present in a great degree not only in drug addicts but also in alcoholics, kleptomaniacs, pyromaniacs, gamblers and certain types of perverts.

A close examination of patients whose illnesses are allied with narcissism shows that at a given moment they yield to a specific impulse within them that is clamoring for gratification. At this given moment the drug addict has developed no other way of handling the impulse. Neither fear of the law nor concern for others who will be affected deters him. Largely devoid of rational judgment and reasoning, he operates solely under the blind need to gratify the impulse immediately. This is another way of saying that the individual under discussion, in common with many others in society, has a low threshold or tolerance for pain, tension, anxiety, criticism, frustration, etc. Any slight discomfort is magnified by the narcissistic individual into an emergency requiring immediate action. However drastic the action which will restore him to a "normal" state, it is justified in his eyes.

As the drug addict's life pattern and rationale begin to unfold, it becomes more and more apparent that his life adds up to a self-enclosed system wherein he is able to provide his own pleasure. True, he must obtain the drugs and administer them, but then he passively awaits the desired effects. He thus isolates himself beyond the need for human help or satisfaction. He is dependent on no other person. Drugs in effect take the place of wife, doctor, priest, friend; but the addict, untrue to life, retains mastery over them all. Turning to no one for help, he becomes his own savior.

In this light, the drugs take on a new significance; they become the aggressor and do all the work. Once he has plunged the needle, the drugs give him what other men spend their lives working for: a feeling of power, a sense of security, sexual satisfaction, and so on. He feels completely at peace with himself and the world. He has succeeded in killing two birds with one stone: maintaining his passivity and withdrawnness while at the same time experiencing the feelings of satisfaction that come to the aggressor.

It should be pointed out that these psychological descriptions of the drug addict are not universally accepted. Those with a more organic approach to the problem believe that the pharmacological needs created by the drugs are in and of themselves a sufficient explanation for his lifelong pursuit of them. In the face of such a strong physiological dependency, all other motivations of necessity assume a lesser importance and do not necessarily reflect immature emotional drives.

Self-Esteem

No matter what the theoretical orientation of workers in the field of drug addiction, they all agree that the addict's self-esteem is very low indeed. The normal person who regards himself in a favorable light neither is destroyed by occasional failures nor does he run away from possible rejections. He operates on the principle that through application he is likely to get a great deal of what he wants in life. But the drug addict, with no confidence in his own capabilities, is caught in a vicious cycle: his low self-esteem prevents him from functioning in society for a sufficient period of time to have successful experiences which would disprove his inner self-attitudes. And if he does not have any outward successful experiences, there is little chance for his self-esteem to be raised. There are those who believe that the problem of drug addiction resolves itself into a simple formula in which the factors are individuals who find only in drugs their lacking self-esteem.

On casual observance the drug addict does not reveal his low self-esteem but may instead appear cocky and boastful. His life is seen as a perpetual denial that he has any such low opinion of himself. However, the history of his work and school life is likely to show the extreme pathological degree of his self-devaluation. One patient based his loss of interest in school and his subsequent truancy on a classroom teacher who laughed at his spelling. Having been singled out as an object of ridicule before the whole class, as he put it, he felt unable to compete further. Another addict was doing well at his job in the garment industry and liked it. But when his employer hired an additional man to help him with the work load, he interpreted his employer's friendliness to the new man as a rejection of himself. Unable to compete with the new worker on a satisfactory basis, he quit his job. It is easy to understand how individuals who withdraw from such imagined slights must feel on becoming caught up in the real double-dealing and trickery of procuring drugs. Their already sagging self-esteem sinks to a new low.

Until not long ago, detailed reports of psychiatric interviews with drug addicts under treatment have been scarce in the literature. However, quite recently two excellent and informative papers have been presented.[9, 10] Each illustrates a method of treating drug addiction, one by what I call the ambulatory hospital method, and the other on an out-patient basis in private psychiatric practice. Each case is a practical illustration of the typical problems and reactions described here: self-destructiveness, immaturity, inability to relate except in terms of dependency, low tolerance for pain or frustration and low self-esteem. In both cases, as the treatment progressed successfully, the patients took a plunge into a mature love relationship. Describing the fears attending these real attempts to react to others, the therapists point out the addict's great need for meaningful social and sexual relationships. Savitt[9] felt that his patient's developing maturity made it possible to substitute sexual activity for addiction. And indeed his patient was able to go on to a more mature relationship and eventually marry.

Successful psychiatric treatment of a drug addict is predicated on the therapist's initial permissiveness of addiction.[8, 9, 11] It is not only futile but fatal even to suggest that an addict give up his strong emotional need for drugs before he has an emotionally satisfying substitute for them.

Idealized Self-Image

The patients at Lexington have a favorite wheeze for the professional staff: "Watch out where you're goin', Doc, or you might get run over by one of the Cadillacs around here." It refers to the fact that so many addicts talk about a Cadillac— either having owned one in the past, owning one at present, or intending to own one. Manifestations of material wealth are of such major importance in their lives that the need for material possessions borders on panic. Dating from their early childhood, it is a direct reflection of their mothers' attitude toward their fathers' ability to provide. An addict's fondest dream is to have a wallet stuffed with big denomination bills, thirty-two suits in his closet, and a Cadillac. In his mind, masculinity and wealth seem to be inextricably linked. The addict respects hard work if it pays off in money but not for the sake of achievement or pure prestige. Addicts who are down and out and have had to pawn their good clothes go to great lengths to avoid their friends. If they don't appear affluent they fear their friends will reject and ridicule them. It is incomprehensible to them that everyone else is not as intensely interested in material things as they are. One addict said with great sympathy and concern, "Doc, you work mighty hard and don't get much money out of it. I could make a lot more than you do every week if I went back to selling drugs."

An intense preoccupation with clothes, money and cars is characteristic of the adolescent group. Although it is a very obvious symptom and the underlying emotions are apparent, in my opinion it is one of the major reasons that adolescents are lured into the drug world. Every adolescent is offered the opportunity to sell drugs, which automatically guarantees him a minimum salary of a hundred dollars per week. Compared to the probable economic circumstances of his family, this is a small fortune. In his unconscious struggle with his father, making real money is concrete proof that he is a better provider and thus a better man.

These materialistic values are, of course, reinforced by group pressure. With money the addict envisions himself in a position of authority in his group, a position he has not hitherto known. With money and an air of bravado he lulls himself into a false sense of independence. He is the little boy in the coonskin cap pretending to be the fearless Davy Crockett. The painful reality is that ultimately he always has to fall back on his family for help—for food, shelter and money. His father remains the strong one and, despite his dreams and his efforts, he loses in the lifelong tug-of-war.

Success and Failure

As we know, the addict is likely to react to a lack of success with near panic. So great is his need for immediate recognition, for *being*, that he does not allow himself a period of *becoming*. He demands of himself success with very little effort. In his competition with other men in the world, he never takes into account their ten years or so of *becoming*. He sees only what other men *have* and he *has not*. Because of his anxiety, he lacks the capacity for long term planning toward a definite goal. So low is his self-esteem that he cannot see himself working hard at a small job with the expectation that it will one day pay off. The thought of working from eight or nine until five or five-thirty for forty-five or so dollars a week is intolerable. Such a job would confirm his feeling that he is a failure. He is incapable of realizing that he would not remain forever in such a job. He cannot take present deprivation in the hope of building toward security in the indefinite future but must continually bolster his self-esteem with immediate proof of present success.

ATTITUDES TOWARD SELF AND OTHERS

Infantile Traits

On analysis, the patterns exhibited by addicts seem to resemble strongly an aspect of early infancy. They are reminiscent of the behavior of a hungry infant whose desperation is appeased only by the breast or bottle. He cannot brook waiting; his demands cannot be tempered. The normal infant grows out of this stage and with increasing awareness comes a realization that he can tolerate his hunger until his bottle is warmed or until other food is prepared. But the drug addict, who has never developed a normal tolerance for hunger or pain, frustration or disappointment, in situations of this kind reacts with the ill-defined tension of the young infant. Fenichel[8] stresses the analogy by pointing out that the addict, like the infant, demands gratification without giving, and that drugs to the addict are as food and warmth to the infant; although the ad-

dict "feeds" himself, he too is passively soothed by the effect
of his "food."

So we see that addicts, in common with all their fellow
creatures, want a feeling of security but attempt to achieve it
by infantile rather than normal adult methods. Preoccupied
with immediate pleasures, they become unduly anxious when
gratification is not immediately forthcoming. The concept of
drug addicts as sexually immature people is entirely compatible
with their pattern of gratification by infantile methods. And
their lack of interest in overt sexuality is logical, for it requires
both stimulation of and interest in someone other than themselves.

The psychoanalytical theory has a reasonable explanation
for this aspect of the addict's behavior. Constantly in the grip
of anxiety, he is incapable of tempering his actions with reality.
Realistic thinking on his own part is impossible; and he cannot
be reached by the realistic thinking of others. The possible
consequences of his actions are of no import. The need must
be gratified to relieve the "pain," and the end justifies the
means.

Psychiatrists, focusing their attention on the preaddiction
personality, believe that there is now sufficient evidence to
warrant such concentration. It seems reasonable to suppose that
in adolescence or young adulthood when the individual must
meet society's demands, the potential addict shows little tolerance for the usual anxieties associated with growing up. Since
he cannot abandon his anxieties he seeks other means of allaying them. By predisposition so little able to tolerate them, he
must act out impulsively. According to this theory, addiction
would be classified with certain psychiatric disturbances known
as impulse disorders.

Hostility

The psychiatrist's early interviews with the addict are
noticeably free of any form of criticism or hostility. This inability to feel or, what is more, express his aggression may be
the root of the addict's problem. It is reasoned that if the addict were able to release his hostility and thus get active pleasure from asserting his rights and expressing his opinions, the

passive pleasures induced by drugs would not be needed. Perhaps because hostility is so inadmissible to the addict, he continually needs drugs to submerge it. One notes that in ordinary situations such as missed appointments or being kept waiting, where the normal person expresses annoyance or even anger, the addict exhibits not the slightest flicker of hostility. If one tacitly gives the patient permission to express himself by saying that his anger is quite justified and quite easy to understand, the thought is intolerable. He may reply, "Why should I be mad? I know you're doing all you can for me." "Anybody can make mistakes." "Who am I to get annoyed about a little thing like that?"

When addicts have had dreams expressing hostility toward the therapist (for example, one in which he is portrayed as a mean and homely person), they have great difficulty bringing themselves to relate such dreams. And if they do, they preface their recital with all manner of explanations, apologies and disavowals.

As the relationship progresses, some anger will be seen to come through, but it is invariably connected with frustration of the patient's dependency wishes. Thus an addict who wanted me to write his term paper took my refusal to mean that I had let him down and was no longer interested in helping him. So great is their inadequacy and helplessness that they are surprised when others don't see them as they see themselves. It is some time before they can realize that refusing to accede to their dependency wishes is not a punishment.

Aggression and Pseudo-aggression

To avoid a mistaken assessment of the emotions of a drug addict, it should be noted that there are two kinds of aggression: so-called healthy aggression and pseudo-aggression. Healthy aggression constitutes those efforts made by an individual which result in bettering his life position; for example, speaking up for himself when misrepresented, asking for a raise when he believes it is justified, going to school to learn a trade in order to get a better position, and the like. A person with healthy aggression may strive to gain an advantageous position in order to show what he can do. His general air of dissatisfaction with his position is coupled with a determination to do something about it.

By contrast, pseudo-aggression is the kind in which the individual's mobilized energies result in defeat. For example, he may take exception to real or imagined mistreatment on a job and make it a matter of principle. Fighting it out means sacrificing his job and his long term goals for the dubious satisfaction of expressing his aggression of the moment. Similarly, pseudo-aggression would include reacting to provocative behavior on the part of an individual known to be disturbed, thereby compounding the emotionally charged situation. The pseudo-aggressive person interprets small incidents in life as large and weighty issues. He feels that his masculinity is threatened if he does not act on them. The drug.addict is unable to sustain and insure his own plans in such a situation because of his need to assert himself. Since almost every job means swallowing many bitter pills, the addict rarely has any work continuity. At the first crisis, however minor, he asserts his independence and walks out.

When an addict describes himself as a strongly aggressive person it will be noted that every instance points to pseudo-aggression rather than healthy aggression, and the end result is to lessen his position in the world. Because of his low self-esteem he continuously walks around with a chip on his shoulder. His assertiveness is never beneficial. Instead he is likely to jeopardize his job or an academic degree because an employer or a teacher has offended him.

Relationship with Parents

Drug addicts seem to have no more and no fewer problems with their parents than the average emotionally disturbed patient. However, there is one characteristic which is found to be always present: the addict so maneuvers himself that he never surpasses his parents in achievements, position or any other way. No matter how poor his family or how extreme his deprivations as a child, his own life is always much worse. Also, the male addict on a conscious level always looks on his father as weak and ineffectual. Fathers are described as cowardly, weak, dominated by their wives and lacking in affection. The addict seems entirely lacking in respect for the parent of the same sex who has neither competed successfully in the world nor with the opposite sex. The addict's bitterness reveals his feeling that in his strong competition with the parent of the same sex he has not won out. This is, of course, quite true, for he has maneuvered himself into an even weaker position than the so-called weak parent.

As therapy continues and the addict's hostility is expressed, another image of the father appears: the strong parent who provides for the family and who has survived the mother's domination. This is the strong image which the patient has felt incapable of living up to or competing with, the image he tries to handle by superficial criticism in an attempt to deny the father's strength, which in truth he feels is completely overwhelming.

These ambivalent attitudes toward his father are the ones the addict carries over to include all subsequent authorities: teachers, employers, physicians, etc. He tries to find his place in the family and to increase his own self-esteem by belittling the father's work efforts and his job. The primary impairment of the addict's self-esteem seems to stem from his inability to identify with the father and feel his own strength in the relationship.

As unwavering as his conscious depiction of the father as a weakling is the addict's deep appreciation of his mother and sympathy for her as an individual and as a victim of his father. In describing any home situation the addict is most sensitive to the mother's suffering and little concerned with the father's in the same situation. Frequently the patient echoes the mother's attitudes toward the father and one senses that the mother has found in the son an ally against the father. Mother and son are often very close and the mother is inclined to be overprotective of him—a perfect way to foster a so-called mother fixation. The patient's evaluation of the father is through the mother's eyes. In marginal economic level homes from which many addicts come, the father usually has long working hours. Instead of giving him credit for his arduous work efforts, the patient echoes the mother's refrain: father has to work such long hours to make a meager living because he is a failure. In this complex and highly charged atmosphere the boy is further estranged from his father.

Repressed Exhibitionism

As can be expected with people who choose a drug which makes them feel withdrawn, drug addicts have a problem with normal exhibitionistic tendencies. From early childhood they overreact to what people may find out, think and say about them. At about nine or ten, when many children are ashamed of their parents, drug addicts often report a shame so acute as to be painful. Their childhood remembrances are of people laughing at them, singling them out for criticism or rebuke. The resulting withdrawal on their part, coupled with the fear that their own feelings and limitations would become known, forced them in childhood to live their lives in fantasy.

Dr. Winklestein's patient[10] treated for heroin addiction was in love with a high school classmate for three years, even though he spoke to her only once. The drug addict is never comfortable unless he can exhibit himself as precisely his proto-type of the successful man.

His need for success makes him withdraw from all activi-ties, for he can't take the chance that he might fail in any of them. School becomes a tortuous affair, unsure as he is of the teachers' reactions and of his own ability to appear as he would like. He shuns any situation which he cannot control and in which he may be exposed in an unfavorable light. Appearing to have no interest in what he is doing is a face-saving device; in case he should fail it would seem that he couldn't care less. He ridicules students who are not afraid of showing their seri-ousness and their anxiety about possible failure, and isolates himself from this stable element.

As a substitute he finds a group with a different set of values, one which respects daring and bravado, one in which he can control the outcome of his behavior. To win over this group he is willing to be the sacrificial lamb; he volunteers to accept any dare made to the group, and in a short time he can exhibit himself in the role of a "big shot." In this new role he must keep well hidden any serious desires involving love, marriage and success in the conventional sense. Caught up in the image he has created, he must live up to his friends' expectations of his role. In this connection I am reminded of an adolescent drug addict's recounting of his secret and involved plans to go to the public library to read some books that interested him. He lived in dread that these excursions would be discovered by his gang.

Combined with his own secret anxieties and desires there is the ever-present temptation to explore the exciting and forbidden things in life. Many addicts, aware of this strong lure, express the belief that if drugs were to be legally administered, as to sick people, adolescents would have no desire to take them; but as long as they are forbidden, the addict will meet the challenge of defying the law to get them. Acquiring the forbidden has given the addict another chance to achieve a feeling of superiority over others, and by outwitting the authorities he can look on himself as their superior in intelligence and resourcefulness. It is natural for adolescents to sample forbidden pleasures, but whereas the average youth is content with a sample, the addict builds his life around activities beyond the pale of society.

REFERENCES

1. Pfeffer, A. Z., and Ruble, D. C.: Chronic psychoses and addiction to morphine. Arch. Neurol & Psychiat. *56:* 665, 1945.
2. Wikler, A.: Drug addiction. In Tice's Practice of Medicine, vol. 8. Hagerstown, Prior, 1953, Pp. 17-49.
3. Brown, R. R., and Partington, J. E.: Intelligence of the narcotic drug addict. J. Gen. Psychol. *26:* 175-179, 1942.
4. Knight, R. C., and Prout, C. T.: A study of results in hospital treatment of drug addictions. Am. J. Psychiat. *108:* 303-308, 1951.
5. Pescor, Michael J.: A Statistical Analysis of the Clinical Records of Hospitalized Drug Addicts. Public Health Reports, Supp. 143, 1943.
6. U. S. Treasury Department, Bureau of Narcotics. Tariffic in Opium and Other Dangerous Drugs. Washington, U. S. Government Printing Office. Published annually.
7. Zimmering, P., et. al.: Heroin addiction in adolescent boys. J. Nerv. & Ment. Dis. *114:* 19-34, 1951.

8. Fenichel, O.: The Psychoanalytic Theory of Neurosis. New York, W. W. Norton, 1945, Pp. 375-386.

9. Savitt, Robert A.: Extramural psychoanalytic treatment of a case of narcotic addiction. J. Am. Psychoanalyt. A. 2: 494-502, 1954.

10. Winkelstein, Charles.: Psychotherapy of a borderline schizophrenic with heroin addiction. Presented before the society for Clinical Psychiatry, Hillside Hospital, Mar. 1955. (To be published in the Journal of the Hillside Hospital.)

11. Simmel, E.: Psychoanalytic treatment in a clinic. Internat. J. Psychoanal. 10: 70-89. 1929.

12. Wikler, A. and Rasor, R.: Psychiatric aspects of drug addiction. Am. J. Med. 14: 566-570, 1953.

13. Kolb, L.: Drug addiction and its relation to crime. Men. Hyg. 9: 74, 1935.

14. Wikler, A.: A psychodynamic study of a patient during experimental self-regulated re-addiction to morphine. Psychiat. Quart. 26: 270-293, 1952.

15. Brown, R. R.: The effect of morphine upon the Rorschach pattern in post-addicts, Am. J. Orthopsychat. 13: 339-342, 1943.

16. Lindesmith, A. R.: Opiate Addiction. Bloomington, Principia Press, 1947.

V. Social Pathology

IT WOULD, OF COURSE, be most helpful to find common denominators in drug addiction which would furnish clues to the underlying causes. But in this particular illness it is virtually impossible to generalize with any degree of safety. No sooner has a set of statistics pointing to certain determinants been released than another comes along revealing quite different results. Each set of findings is valid for the group under observation, but few, if any, general conclusions can be drawn from the various studies. Neither intelligence, social stratum, occupation, religion nor race seems to have any bearing on drug addiction. So far, the only gaugeable common denominators are the actual physiological and pharmacological results of taking drugs.

Although workers in the field constantly refer to "the typical drug addict," the term is meaningless. It usually refers to the addict whose record is in the courts. Without question, here is one type of addict, but the public and the lawmakers have been misled by this neat and simple categorization. They have directed their thinking toward rehabilitating this so-called typical addict and have thereby excluded many other types who do not fit the picture at all.

The data from various studies presented below hold true only for the specific groups from which they are drawn. Many of the data are subject to interpretation; other isolated facts and figures do not fall within any known psychological or social theories. Despite its disconnected form, this information is part and parcel of the total knowledge of drug addiction. Only by increasing, sifting and dovetailing such information will a clearer and fuller understanding of the whole problem come about. Each set of findings will be presented for its individual interest and worth, rather than for its relevance to any particular sociological theory of drug addiction.

83

Social data on drug addicts are very limited, the bulk coming from the records at Lexington Hospital. It is true that Lexington has some voluntary patients, but the majority are there for varying lengths of time as prisoners or probationary prisoners. The follow-up studies which furnish the statistics on relapse and cure are based on probation officers' reports. Once a patient is discharged or paroled, he is required to see his probation officer at least once a month and he cannot leave the vicinity without permission during his probation, which may be up to five years. Discharged patients who are not subsequently arrested for any major or minor criminal acts are assumed to be off drugs. This fairly safe assumption is based on a long history of arrests, invariably traceable to the patient's need for money to buy drugs. It is nevertheless clear that neither remaining in touch with his probation officer nor avoiding any skirmishes with the law constitutes positive proof that a patient has not relapsed to drugs. In fact, he might relapse on the day of his release and be able to stay on the right side of the law for a year or more, in which case his record would give a false picture of the length of abstinence. This inevitable inaccuracy accounts for the wide differences in estimated cures—from 2 per cent to as high as 25 per cent.

However, an intelligent and constructive drug control program, worked out by physicians, local law enforcement agencies and other interested groups, does not hinge on the exactitude of such figures. It is important to agree on certain basic truths and to realize that the percentage of cures lies somewhere within this wide range. It is impossible to plan a program, make laws and foresee what money will be needed without some statistical data. Should the laws be revised, enabling addicts to come out of hiding, physicians will be able to contribute accurate statistics on this illness just as on any other. With a pooling of experiences and collecting of facts, existing programs can be modified to meet the country's needs. Until such time we can broaden our scope by working with the best estimates at hand.

INCIDENCE

The difficulties inherent in estimating the incidence of drug addiction in the general population of the United States are further augmented by outside factors. Estimates are bound to be influenced by the interests and orientation of the people who make them. Thus the lowest estimates come from those whose goal of success is measured by a decrease in drug addiction throughout the country. As we have seen in Chapter I, the U. S. Bureau of Narcotics has given out an approximate figure; surveys conducted under its auspices indicate 60,000 addicts in the United States or one addict per 3000 population. This study showed a marked decrease in addiction since 1924. Shortly after World War I (1924) the U. S. Public Health Service conducted a study which indicated that there was one addict per 1000 population. In 1945 it was reported that approximately one draftee in 10,000 was rejected for military service primarily because of drug addiction.

A Detroit civic committee for the study of drug addiction in 1931 found that there were 511 addicts legally supplied with drugs and 734 addicts using illegal drugs out of a population of approximately 1,568,662. Applying these figures to the country at large would mean that there were roughly 76 addicts per 100,000 population as of that year. The New York City Mayor's Committee in 1951, reviewing the local drug problem, estimated from police records that there were 90,000 addicts in New York City alone out of almost 8,000,000, or approximately one out of every 87 inhabitants.

Hospital, church, school and youth activity workers report a marked increase in addiction within their respective groups. A Harlem minister gives the alarming report that within twenty years addiction in his parish has increased from a negligible percentage to the point where one out of every four of his families is involved. In private practice I would estimate that perhaps one out of every six drug addict patients has had an encounter with the law. It can readily be seen from these scattered figures that estimates of drug addicts in the United States range from approximately 60,000 to 1,000,000.

The lack of any accurate statistics makes it extremely difficult to push through legislative programs or to work on the related sociological problems. In fact, the control of any medical
illness begins with the accumulation of reliable statistics. After
seeing in black and white the scope and range of the illness,
those in charge can map out what to do about it and how to do
it. The incidence of drug addiction and its related social factors are of paramount importance in countrywide planning,
both legislative and otherwise. Available data from local surveys as well as data on drug addicts who have run afoul of the
law obviously leave wide gaps. To what extent are these local
surveys representative of the whole country? Is there not a
decided tendency to underestimate the number of addicts in
the higher economic strata?

Many of the methods used to determine the incidence of
addiction where there is no legal proof amount to guesses at
best. They depend on using the number of addicts treated or
arrested as representing a certain percentage of the addict population and, when drug peddlers are arrested, estimating how
many addicts each supplies, etc.

The Bureau of Narcotics also bases estimates on the
amount of illicit drugs seized. It was reported that the total
amount of opium seized dropped from 3300 ounces in 1945
to 789 ounces in 1951. Amounts of heroin seized showed an
increase in 1949 and dropped in the following year. Basing
the incidence of addiction on drug seizures would seem to leave
numerous loopholes. It has been suggested that a decrease in
seizures, despite an increase in police activity, may be due to
the smugglers' enforced change in smuggling methods, i.e.,
smaller quantities at a time, so that correspondingly small
quantities turn up at each police seizure. It does not require
great shrewdness on the part of a smuggler to realize that putting all his eggs in one basket is not good business. Certainly
the increase in adolescent addiction is not compatible with the
assumed decrease in black-market heroin.

Even the evidence that drug addiction has decreased in
certain states where stringent laws have been passed against
peddlers is open to doubt. People working in this field say that

addicts simply move on to areas where the punishment is less severe. Many states are actively attacking the problem of drug addiction by passing laws carrying heavy penalties, yet there is no question that addiction has been on a steady increase in this country in the past five years. The total prison and hospital populations have shown up to a 300 per cent increase in drug addicts in this period, and members of narcotics squads speak of "epidemic proportions." According to Dr. Vogel (U.S.P.H.S.),[13] Lexington and Fort Worth, the two U. S. Public Health Service hospitals, in 1950 admitted a total of 440 addicts under 21 years of age, as compared with 22 in this age group in 1947. The impossibility of gauging the rate of increase in drug addiction is most unfortunate all around. Physicians, social workers, educators, legislators and others are trying to bring under control an epidemic whose proportions are unknown.

Ratio of Male to Female Addicts

The ratio of male to female addicts has changed radically since the Harrison Narcotic Act went into effect. Before the handling of narcotics became a criminal act there were many more female addicts than male; in fact, the ratio was roughly estimated to be two to one. It would seem that when narcotics could be obtained legally, women used them freely to relieve physical or mental distress; indeed many became medically addicted in this way. On the other hand, men used narcotics then much as they do now—purely for the pleasure and thrill-giving effect. With the advent of the Harrison Act in 1914, women addicts seem to have responded to the strong public sentiment against narcotics, for their number has rapidly decreased until the present ratio is believed to be one female to three or four males.

Dr. Kolb, writing on "Drug Addiction Among Women,"[14] says that according to the figures "women have respect for as well as fear of the law." His analysis of the nature of crimes committed by addicts reveals that men are eighteen times as likely to become involved in vicious crimes as women—a statement borne out by the experiences of others. Yet female addicts seem to sink to a much lower level of degradation than male addicts. It may be that males can better withstand the degrading effects or perhaps they do not represent as socially deteriorated a type as the females who succumb to drugs. In prisons, state reformatories or houses of detention, the female addict population is largely made up of women arrested primarily for prostitution, drunk rolling or petty thievery. The women patients I saw at Lexington in 1946 were beyond question a far more unstable and unruly group than the men.

Race

The ethnic background of drug addicts varies from one part of the country to another, paralleling general population trends. Lexington's records and those coming from the country as a whole seem to show that no race is preponderantly susceptible to drug addiction. Regarding the common misconception that drug addiction is more prevalent among Negroes, Lambert[1] in 1930 stated that there were eight Negro addicts to 310 white addicts—roughly 2.5 per cent, although Negroes made up almost 10 per cent of the population. He also noted that in upwards of three-fourths of the group studied, the majority of addicts were native born. In his study of 318 addicts, 275 were born in the United States, 15 were from Puerto Rico, 9 from Central America and 19 from various European countries.

Treadway,[2] in a detailed social analysis of 1660 addicts, also found that the majority of addicts were native born and had native born parents. The California State Narcotics Committee in 1931 reported on 624 cases: 47 per cent included those of Anglo-Saxon origin, Latin and Negro; 27.7 per cent were Chinese and 25.1 per cent Mexican. Pescor[3] notes that the percentage of foreign born among addicts at Lexington is lower by 11.6 per cent than in the population at large. A study of 47 typical physician addicts revealed that they were predominantly native born but of foreign born parents.[4]

Occupation

To obtain a valid comparison of addiction percentages by occupation is virtually impossible inasmuch as economic and other factors in each local group surveyed are bound to weight the results. Practically all of the patients in private hospitals are from upper middle class or at least better than average homes. Of the 318 addicts at Bellevue, studied by Lambert,[1] occupations were various; there were 62 laborers, 31 salesmen, 27 clerks, 18 waiters, 16 painters, 12 seamen, and so on. In a series of 100 female addicts, however, trained nurses made up the largest professional group. Pescor[4] found that the proportion of physicians in the addict group was approximately eight times that of physicians in the general population. It has long been recognized that a disproportionately large number of doctors and nurses become addicted, no doubt because of the easy availability of drugs. In countries such as England which do not have a flourishing underworld-dominated black market in drugs, physicians make up a considerable majority of the addict population.

The economic adjustment of addicts is fairly predictable: they are much more likely to be employed irregularly or not at all than to be steadily and gainfully employed. Incidentally, the physician who becomes addicted after he is well established professionally usually continues to maintain a satisfactory economic adjustment. But early addiction invariably interferes with or halts the pursuit of education as well as any trade or skill requiring application and experience to become adept. For this reason, the drug addict is likely to live in marginal economic circumstances.

The Narcotic Educational Association of Michigan reports that of 83 addicts studied in 1936, 64 were shoplifters. Only 9 were gainfully employed and 2 were maintained by relatives. However, in another survey of 1049 addicts (Chicago), 82 per cént were regularly employed and 18 per cent irregularly employed.[5] Pescor's report shows that the majority of hospitalized addicts do their work when off drugs. Approximately 10 per cent of them are either unable or unwilling to work, or shirk their responsibilities.

A study made of the parents of drug addicts at Lexington showed that 57 per cent were of a marginal economic status, 37 per cent were in comfortable circumstances.

Religion

There is little reliable information as to the relationship between religious background and addiction, although some comparative studies have been made. The majority of drug addicts report that they gave up church attendance when they reached adolescence. Pescor's breakdown of the religious training of patients at Lexington in 1945 is as follows: 45.2 per cent Protestant, 25.4 per cent Catholic, 24.8 per cent no preference, 4.1 per cent Jewish, .5 per cent other religions. Other studies conducted by Dai in Chicago and Jandy and Floch in Detroit reveal a higher percentage of Catholics. In Lambert's study of 318 addicts at Bellevue in 1930, 193 were Catholic, 63 were Protestant and 62 Jewish. The fluctuation throughout the country seems to reflect local concentrations of the different religious groups, and in all probability the Lexington figures are a more accurate index to the religious background of addicts throughout the country.

Education

The educational level of drug addicts is roughly comparable to that of the general population—i.e., a grade school education. However, a breakdown reveals that female addicts have a slight educational edge over males, a fact which lends support to the theory that women are more likely to become addicted as a result of needs arising from their personal weaknesses than through association with retrograded types.

MARITAL STATUS AND ADDICTION

No clear linking of marital status to addiction emerges from the various surveys. At Lexington it was found that many addicts described their status as married, although the legality of the relationship was questionable. In all probability a considerable number were common law marriages in which they assumed little responsibility, so that it is difficult to decide on the proper classification. In several studies, over 50 per cent of the addicts under observation were classified as single. Kolb's study of 119 self-designated medical addicts[15] revealed 79 who were married, 25 who were separated or divorced and 15 who were single. Pescor's study showed that the typical physician addict was married and had two children on the average.

HOME BACKGROUND OF ADDICTS

The influence of the home in setting the social values of the growing child has long been recognized and physicians have therefore been particularly interested in the home background of drug addicts. Kolb states that in more than half .of his "medical" addicts there was evidence of psychosis, neurosis or alcoholism in near relatives. Other studies bolster the conclusion that families of drug addicts are more emotionally unstable than other families. But any such figures are difficult to assess and to compare with the population as a whole. In any event, the difference may be insignificant in view of the large percentage of emotionally disturbed patients in the general population as revealed by reports from hospital out-patient clinics.

In regard to family structure and relationships, the physician addict's history differs from that of other addicts in that his home was generally intact and had a congenial atmosphere. The manifest difficulties in gauging one's own environment must, of course, be borne in mind. In a series of women addicts, about half had left home by the age of 16—an indication that the home environment was in all probability not very favorable.

Pescor's 1943 report[3] shows that of the 1036 addicts studied, 54 per cent were reared by both parents, 14.5 per cent by the mother only, 2 per cent by the father only, and the remaining raised by step-parents or institutions. In analyzing the continuity of the home he found that 55 per cent of the patients had an intact home until they reached the age of 18; 15 per cent had lost their fathers by death and 9 per cent had lost their mothers; 6 per cent had lost both parents and 15 per cent came from separated and divorced homes. Of this group, 47 per cent enjoyed a congenial home life and average discipline; 26 per cent described the family discipline as poor. According to their own evaluation, 77 per cent of the 1,036 patients had apparently normal family relationships; 11 per cent had loose famliy ties; 3 per cent had a mother fixation and 9 per cent had a hatred for either a parent or step-parent.

In a study of private patients[6] at New York Hospital it was found that 26 out of 75 addicts exhibited close parental attachment, 23 to their mothers. The position of the child in the family seems to have little bearing on drug addiction. In a study of 97 women addicts in the Chicago Women's Reformatory, 25 per cent were youngest children in the family; 19 per cent were the oldest; 16 per cent were only children and 24 per cent occupied other intermediate positions.

From the foregoing scattered statistics it seems clear that there is no outstanding characteristic in the family structure which predisposes a member toward drug addiction. Similarly, there seems to be no obvious relationship between the drug addict's family structure and his attitude toward marriage—willingness to enter into it or avoidance of it.

CAUSES OF ADDICTION

From the sociological point of view it is necessary to differentiate between the causes of the first trial of drugs and the causes of addiction. Unfortunately, there are no statistics covering those individuals in the general population who try drugs one or more times but do not become addicts.

Initiation to drugs usually occurs in a social situation and hence the habit may be considered a socially acquired one. Studies of adolescent groups in particular demonstrate the social patterns which over a period of time foster the use of drugs consistently enough to cause addiction. Dai[5] found that the addicts he studied first acquired information about drugs through associating with drug users. He classifies the types of social situation which resulted in the initial encounter with drugs as follows: pleasure parties; association with prostitutes and pimps; pool rooms and gambling houses; association with co-workers in hotels and restaurants; contact with drug peddlers; contact with homosexuals.

Zimmering[9] in a study of twenty-two adolescent male heroin addicts found that they were introduced to the drug by peddlers and other users. He concluded that addicts try to initiate their friends in order to decrease their own guilt feelings and also to increase their number of potential suppliers. He further pointed out that curiosity about forbidden pleasures is a strong factor in the adolescent's initial use of drugs.

Physician addicts almost invariably report that they first used drugs to relieve pain. Female addicts also tend to give relief of pain as their reason, whereas male addicts report association with drug users and/or curiosity.

An interesting theory of the cause of addiction, based on conclusions drawn from an intensive study of 60 addicts, has been advanced by Lindesmith.[7] He suggests that individuals given narcotics in hospitals who experience withdrawal symptoms and are told the reason for these symptoms are likely to become addicted. Conversely, hospitalized patients who become medically addicted and suffer withdrawal symptoms are unlikely to take up drugs after their illness if they are ignorant of the cause of their pain and of how it can be relieved.

Lindesmith considers the patient's attitude toward the drug during the period of use rather than his motive for initially using the drug, to be the determining factor in addiction. If the individual does not perceive that his distress is due to withdrawal he cannot become addicted; if he does, addiction is quickly and permanently established. Once the patient realizes that he may be addicted to narcotics, his attitude is one of self-condemnation.

Further experience with the drug's releasing of pain and tension serves to convince him that he has become a "dope fiend." It is this self-impression which transforms a non-addict into an addict and Lindesmith considers the transformation to be largely a matter of semantics: the individual who "uses the symbols which society provides him also assumes the attitudes appropriate to those symbols when he applies them to himself. He calls himself a dope fiend and gradually hardens himself to the fact that he has become an outcast and a pariah . . ."

Dai[5] found among supposed medical cases remarkable support for the theory that it is their knowledge of the narcotic that is a determining factor in addiction, whereas his study of physician addicts suggested to Pescor that it is their knowledge of what drugs can do for tired or tense patients that predisposes them to try drugs themselves.

At the present time it is safe to say that the average initial contact with drugs is not a medical one. With a widening knowledge of the dangers involved, fewer and fewer people are becoming addicted in this way. In a United States Bureau of Narcotics report[10] (1935) on 946 narcotic users who were arrested, the following reasons for addiction were given: 486, association with addicts; 337, illness or injury; 50, indulgence or drink; 14, mental strain; 10, curiosity.

The reasons or rationalizations given by drug addicts for their initial use of drugs have been subjected to varied interpretations and indeed it is impossible to gauge to what extent they can be considered valid interpretations. Before 1930 the addict's rationalizing of his habit as an aftermath of the therapeutic use of drugs was accepted as a corollary of the physician's widespread and indiscriminate prescribing of narcotics. But present-day indications are that the major cause of addiction is association with drug addicts. So we must logically ask why potential addicts of the present day seek out such companions: do they have an abnormal curiosity? And if so, why?

Another common rationalization is that drugs were first used to relieve hangovers. There is no question that many a relapse to drugs follows excessive indulgence in alcohol. Statistics from Lexington show that 30 per cent of the patients relapsed because of association with addicts, or to recapture a thrill; 17 per cent relapsed to relieve pain or discomfort; 16 per cent relapsed after alcoholic sprees.

Another study[5] indicates that relapse was coincidental with and probably due to the patient's incapacity to face the demands of the normal life situations in our culture. The patients with the best chance for permanent cure appear to be those who adjust satisfactorily to institutional life, and on leaving the hospital have a home and employment awaiting them, as well as adequate supervision during and after the difficult transition to their new way of life.

ONSET OF ADDICTION

Although the age at which an individual becomes addicted is dependent to a large extent on existing social and environmental factors, in the medical literature there are cases of addiction occurring in early childhood and others occurring as late as the mid-seventies, resulting from drug intake during medical illness.

Studies in 1928 and 1929 established the average age of addiction as somewhere between 20 and 30, but the present bustling black market is reaching increasing numbers of adolescents so that the median is now undoubtedly lower. On the other hand, the average physician addict, according to Pescor,[4] began using drugs at the age of 39. A study made in the Chicago area[5] in 1937 showed that females tend to become addicted at an earlier age than males, and that the period between initial exposure to drugs and the establishment of addiction ranged from one week to five years.

Statistics on the age of beginning addiction of patients in private hospitals[6] differ widely from those covering patients at Lexington.[3] A report on 75 private patients admitted to New York Hospital over a twenty-year period (1930–1950) shows the average age at which they began using drugs to be 37.2 years. A breakdown of the Lexington figures shows that 16 per cent began using drugs at the age of 19 or under; 28 per cent between the ages of 20 and 24; 25 per cent between the ages of 25 and 29; 14 per cent between the ages of 30 and 34 and 17 per cent over the age of 35. This discrepancy suggests that social and economic factors must play a part in determining the age of beginning addiction. It also points to the conclusion that the lower economic classes have earlier experiences with drugs and are either more susceptible to them, or the drugs are more available to young people in this group than in the middle or upper economic classes.

PERCENTAGE OF CURES

The term cure as applied to drug addicts is a misnomer, just as with alcoholics. Technically, a cured addict could not relapse from his state of non-addiction by taking a single shot of a narcotic. But since cure in drug addiction means simply total abstinence, the first shot of morphine to an ex-addict is like the first drink to an ex-alcoholic. Because of this fact, any surgical treatment he may require carries the hazard of a return to his former addiction. Aware of this danger, Danny Carlson, founder and moving force in Narcotics Anonymous, who is himself a former addict, refused to take any narcotics whatsoever when one of his lungs was removed because of carcinoma.

As we have seen earlier in the chapter, estimates on the percentage of cures are as unreliable as those on the incidence of drug addiction. As Lexington these estimates are, at best, guesses based on several factors. Patients are considered cured who do not return to the hospital for further treatment; who are not arrested after their release (the F.B.I. notifies Lexington authorities of any arrests); who have clean records with their probation officers. It is clear that any such evidence is negative in nature and inconclusive on the face of it, but the clandestine nature of the whole drug addiction picture precludes a more thorough and efficient check.

Throughout the country one finds estimates of cures ranging from 2 per cent to 25 per cent. As at Lexington and Fort Worth, the authorities must rely largely on prison and police records as evidence of an addict's relapse to drugs. Thus the abstinence period is roughly estimated to be the elapsed time between discharge from the hospital, and/or prison, and the first subsequent arrest. The experience of private physicians is that the majority of patients taking involuntary cures relapse within one day to one month after discharge.

In order to understand the total picture of the addict's efforts either to cure himself or to reduce his dosage, we shall briefly discuss the four phases involved: length of addiction, number of treatments attempted; rate of relapse and length of abstinence.

LENGTH OF ADDICTION, TREATMENT
AND RELAPSE

Because of the low rate of cures, the length of addiction in most cases may be considered to extend from the onset of the habit throughout the addict's entire lifetime. Statistics are based on the interval between his reported initial addiction and the time he comes under observation. Lambert[1] reports a range of one to fifty years for patients voluntarily undergoing treatment at Bellevue Hospital. Pescor[4] found the addiction of physicians to be thirteen years on the average—a figure compatible with their late age of beginning addiction, which was 39 years. A report of the Welfare Council of New York City in 1951 indicates that adolescent addicts are being apprehended earlier; 61 adolescent drug addicts out of 115 had been using narcotics for less than six months at the time of observation.

Drug addicts characteristically undergo numerous cures—in state and city hospitals, private sanitoria and Public Health Service hospitals. Although they insist that these hospitalizations represent attempts at cure, it has been pointed out earlier that many addicts desire merely to reduce their dosage in order to avoid the difficulties and expense of keeping up a strong habit. The number of attempted treatments varies with the length of addiction. Then, too, a patient who has spent two or three years in prison will not have as long a record of attempted cures as one who has never been arrested.

A study of 120 female addicts in New York City, made in 1929,[11] reveals that 15 had been treated once, 24 twice, 20 three times, 17 four times, 15 five times, and 29 had had up to twelve hospitalizations. Lambert estimates that the average number of attempted cures is four, but patients seen in private practice seem to have a slightly higher average.

Dai in his Chicago study[5] compares the number of treatments attempted by law violators and by other addicts in hospitals who have not run afoul of the law. In the series of hospital cases, 41 per cent had had more than one previous medical treatment as opposed to 5 per cent of the law violators. These figures are consistent with the difference in attitude toward addiction of the patients who return involuntarily to

Lexington time after time, and those who manage to stay on the right side of the law and seek private help.

Physician addicts show an average of three voluntary attempts at cure in their average 13 year addiction.[4]

Lindesmith's study[7] indicates that all chronic users at one time or another attempt to abstain from drugs. Unfortunately, over-all statistics covering this phase do not indicate whether treatment was voluntary or involuntary, whether the motive was to effect a cure or to reduce the dosage of drugs.

The over-all relapse figures from various sources are quite high. Lambert[1] reveals that 88 per cent of the 318 addicts he studied had previously taken cures and relapsed. The California Senate Committe report of 1936 shows that 81 per cent of its discharged patients relapsed within the sixteen-month parole period following treatment. In a six-month follow-up study of drug addict physicians who had received treatment, Pescor[4] found that 50 per cent were still off drugs; 27 per cent had relapsed; and no information was available on the remaining 23 per cent. Pescor[8] attempted to check up on 4776 male patients six months after their discharge from Lexington. He was able to determine that 39 per cent had relapsed; 13 per cent were still abstinent; 7 per cent had died, and he could not determine the status of the other 41 per cent.

As can readily be seen, the statistics on length of abstinence, derived from studying addicts who have relapsed following cures and those who have never abstained, do not take into account the unknown number of once addicted individuals who have taken themselves off drugs. In a two-month study of the general medical population of New York's Bellevue Hospital for the purpose of uncovering patients with a previous history of addiction who were clearly not presently addicted, I found seven such cases. They had been addicted from ten to twenty years earlier and all of them had voluntarily gone off drugs either for economic reasons or because they disliked the drug addict's way of life. They showed little or no interest in the whole problem and did not consider the possibility of relapse. Their attitude had little in common with that of individuals more recently off drugs and still feeling very vulnerable. These seven people had either forgotten the once overpowering pull or had so firmly rejected drugs as to render them no longer a temptation. In any event, the study of similar groups from general hospitals, trade unions, etc.—delving into their attitudes and personality adjustments in relation to drugs —would undoubtedly turn up some of the answers to the ever-present problem of relapse.

VOLUNTARY TREATMENT

There is considerable difference of opinion as to what conditions favor rehabilitation of the drug addict: whether voluntary or involuntary, patients are most likely to continue to abstain from drugs after treatment. Studies of both types of patients were made at Lexington, where the experience with the voluntary group was very poor. These patients stayed from one day to three months, invariably signing out against medical advice. Although it was obvious that they were not seeking a cure but merely a reduction in drug intake, statistically they were classified as voluntary patients. Considering the large turnover in these so-called voluntary patients, it was generally believed that the optimum conditions for a patient to remain abstinent were for him to be hospitalized as a probationary prisoner and discharged on parole.

The big discrepancy in this reasoning lies in the use of the term "voluntary" to describe the admission of patients who actually have no desire to be cured at the time. Instead of using the voluntary and involuntary categories, it would be more reasonable and fair to compare addicts in the most favorable group at Lexington—the probationary group—with private patients who seek help without any pressure from the law. Statistics on this latter group are so scanty that it would be necessary to make broad estimations. But even on the slight evidence, private clinicians working in the field believe that there is a considerably higher percentage of cures among patients who really want to be rid of their addiction, and that the patient's subjective attitude toward drugs is of primary importance in effecting a cure—and thus is a primary element in the total rate of cure.

According to Pescor,[12] the fact that 58 per cent of the patients at Lexington had had compulsory treatments previous to their hospitalization there bears out the old adage: "He that complies against his will is of his own opinion still." He goes on to say that, in general, enforced cures are not as effective as voluntary cures, almost half the patients relapsing in less than one month after release.

Addicts themselves seem to know that their attitude toward addiction is a crucial factor. The spread of Narcotics Anonymous, which has struggled against great odds in its few years of existence, indicates that there is a growing negative attitude toward drug addiction within the ranks. The support given by this organization should not be underestimated. It not only gives individual addicts a helping hand toward their goal of abstinence but, perhaps more importantly, it is a strong force in bringing about a change in their attitude toward drugs.

REFERENCES

1. Lambert A., et. al.: Report of the Mayor's Committee on Drug Addiction. Am. J. Psychiat. *10:* 433-538, 1930.
2. Treadway, W. L.: Further observations on the epidemiology of narcotic drug addiction. Pub. Health Rep. *45:* 541-553, 1930.
3. Pescor, M. J.: A statistical analysis of the clinical records of hospitalized drug addicts. Pub. Health Rep., Suppl. 143, 1943.
4. Pescor, M. J.: Physician drug addicts. Dis. Nerv. Syst. *3:* 173-174, 1942.
5. Dai, Bingham: Opium Addiction in Chicago. Shanghai, Commercial Press, 1937.
6. Knight, Robert C. and Prout, C. T.: A study of results in hospital treatment of drug addictions. Am. J. Psychiat. *108:* 303-308, 1951.
7. Lindesmith, A. R.: Opiate Addiction. Bloomington, Principia Press, 1947.
8. Pescor, Michael, J.: Follow-up study of treated narcotic drug addicts. Pub. Health Rep., Suppl. 170, 1943.
9. Zimmering, P. et. al.: Heroin addiction in adolescent boys. J. Nerv. & Ment. Dis. *114:* 19-34, 1951.
10. U. S. Treasury Department, Bureau of Narcotics. Traffic in opium and other dangerous drugs. Washington, U. S. Government Printing Office, 1935.
11. Magid, M. O.: Narcotic drug addiction in the famale. M. J. & Rec. *129:* 306-310, 1929.
12. Pescor, M. J.: A statistical analysis of the clinical records of hospitalized drug addicts. Pub. Health Rep., Suppl. 143, 1938.
13. Weston, Paul: Narcotics U. S. A. New York, Greenberg, 1952, p. 10.
14. Kolb, Lawrence: Drug addiction among women. Proc. Am. Prison A., pp. 349-357, 1938.
15. Kolb, Lawrence: Drug addiction. A study of some medical cases. Arch. Neurol. & Psychiat, *20:* 171-183, 1928.

VI. Clinical Diagnosis

INITIAL DIFFICULTIES

THE RELATIONSHIP between the physician and the drug addict under our present legal structure is inevitably filled with difficulties, not the least of which is mutual wariness and distrust. The addict who consults a physician is painfully aware of the strict limitations of the law: he knows that the physician cannot legally give an addict drugs. Similarly, the physician's attitude reflects his own frustration: he cannot treat the problem of addiction as a medical illness and is therefore annoyed to find a drug addict in his waiting room. Many authorities in the field deplore these present-day attitudes and believe it would be far better if the physician were allowed freely and legally to take over the management of the drug addict, who would in turn be able to discuss his problem openly without having to resort to subterfuges.

The drug addict's long-established patterns of trickery and conniving are the main deterrents to a correct diagnosis of the illness by the physician in his office. Usually the addict consults a physician for one of the following reasons:

1. He may want to be withdrawn from drugs.
2. He may be actually ill.
3. He may feign illness in order to obtain drugs.
4. He may appeal directly for a prescription, on the basis of his severe withdrawal symptoms.
5. He may want to "case" the office, with a view to stealing narcotics or prescription blanks either at the time or in the future.

The physician is obviously a prime target because he is empowered to dispense precious narcotics, albeit for legal purposes only, so addicts carefully plan to make their illnesses sound plausible. They have also been known to attack physicians, steal and forge prescriptions, in order to obtain drugs.

No matter how carefully the physician may proceed toward making a correct diagnosis, it must be remembered that he is not dealing with an amateur; the typical addict's time and energies are constantly consumed in disguising the true picture. He may build up such a convincing case that the physician will not be able to penetrate its distortions to reach the truth. Then, too, the physician who prescribes drugs to an addict is a marked individual. He is sure to be besieged by other addicts who have heard by the grapevine that he is an easy touch.

A physician recounted to me the case history of a 21 year old woman whose intention to go off drugs seemed entirely sincere. He felt that she merited his help in carrying out her resolution and prescribed methadone for her period of withdrawal. The following day he was confronted with eight drug addicts, all of whom requested methadone for the same purpose. The connection was obvious, but the physician interviewed them all individually instead of dismissing the lot. This creditable act had a reward: one of the group requested hospitalization and was successfully withdrawn from drugs. This incident serves to point up the physician's difficulties. He may put untold energy and effort into rehabilitating drug addicts and naturally resents being "conned."

Needless to say, addicts dedicated to outwitting the physicians they consult are not satisfactory patients. They are not candidates for withdrawal, as they often claim, but are simply making the rounds in the hope of obtaining an inexpensive and sure source of drugs, or even a temporary supply to tide them over from one day to the next. They usually give fictitious names and addresses and rarely pay for consultation.

The purpose of this chapter is to elaborate on the "typical" drug addict's habitual behavior, in particular toward the medical profession. Armed with this knowledge, the physician may save himself needless concern and effort, not to mention some emotional wrenches. It is too much to ask that the physician seek out these patients for treatment but perhaps an awareness of their conniving and deception will help him to maintain his time-honored professional objectivity and sympathetic detachment and thus speed their return to his office for withdrawal treatment. As long as an addict is actively on drugs, with no intention of going off, the physician cannot expect from him either honesty or coöperation or respect for the profession at large.

It is unfortunately true that no laboratory test yet devised will reveal addiction, although there are tests which indicate the presence of narcotics in the body.* These tests, performed by only a few laboratories, do not constitute legal proof of addiction. The physician must therefore depend on certain clues in establishing a correct diagnosis. Understandably, these clues vary widely. Neither the addict's appearance and manner, his behavior, his reaction to illness, nor the physical findings on examination can be said to come within standardized limits.

The whole problem is simplified when an addict frankly admits his addiction—quite a disarming approach to the physician who is used to innumerable subterfuges. However, the frank admission of addiction is often in itself a device calculated to evoke a positive response from the physician. The patient usually goes on to say that he appreciates the physician's position and will never trouble him again. A favorite story is that his regular source of drugs is temporarily cut off and he needs a prescription for a few days' supply; he will under no circumstances, he says, spread the word about the physician's generosity.

In the group of addicts who feign illness, the chief complaint is usually one in which the administration of drugs is medically justified: a gall bladder or kidney stone attack, sciatica, acute abdominal distress, acute coronary thrombosis, as well as a large list of injuries—self-inflicted. The swallowing of safety pins or other sharp objects is a frequently employed ruse. The patient of course expects a shot of morphine before removal of the object: a safety pin in the rectum, for instance.

---

*Although Nalline, as mentioned on pages 27 and 110, is helpful in confirming addiction *in vivo*, there is presently no laboratory test *(in vitro)* that will consistently stand up as legal evidence.

During the history taking, the physician will be struck by several inconsistencies. The addict's description of his severe present illness makes it seem a wonder that he could get to the physician's office under his own power. Questions about previous treatment for this severely painful condition are parried or evaded. As the examination proceeds, the patient's intent usually becomes quite clear. While protesting that he is much too ill to work, he fiercely resists the idea of hospitalization, laboratory procedures or diagnostic tests. He tries to give the impression that his reluctance is based solely on financial considerations, but when he refuses free clinic treatment at a hospital it becomes apparent that he wants no part of any medical work-up. In general, the patient's intensity and exaggeration of symptomatology give him away. On the basis of his own story, immediate hospitalization is indicated. True, the average medical or surgical patient may be frightened of hopitalization or reluctant for reasons of family responsibilities, possible loss of job, etc., but he does not want to continue to live with a painful condition when he has the opportunity to have it cleared up. Not so the addict, who usually refuses any such suggestion.

Added to the dissembling is a further complication for the physician: the actual appearance of illness. We have already mentioned that there are usually no presenting symptoms that will reveal addiction, but the addict's general malnutrition and pallor, coupled with the intense anxiety caused by his precarious pursuit of drugs, sometimes make him appear acutely ill indeed. No matter how experienced the physician, he is bound to be disturbed by this pitiable individual. Under our present laws, giving an addict drugs to alleviate his desperate condition may constitute poor judgment, but the physician's traditional sensitivity to suffering—whatever the cause—makes the task of refusing a difficult one.

The drug addict's history of feigned illness will be fairly accurate as to details. Through the years he may have spent some time in penal institutions; he is undoubtedly familiar with physician's offices; he has compared notes with other addicts. All in all, he has learned a good deal about illness in its many forms and knows that the physician may well accept his trumped-up story, turning his doubts inward rather than toward the patient. A common dodge is for the addict to request medication for a couple of days with the explanation that his own physician, who is out of town, always gives him something to take care of his severe but transient symptoms.

Serious criticism has been leveled against the physician on the grounds that he cannot distinguish malingering from true symptomatology. His lack of experience with drug addicts has been considered sufficient reason for barring him from handling their treatment. To the same extent that this charge is true of general physicians, it is also true of experienced workers in the field of drug addiction, who should, by the same criterion, be well equipped to handle the problems arising from addiction. I know of no physician in this field, however widely experienced, who is not constantly beset with the difficulty of distinguishing between real and simulated illnesses in drug addicts. And I know of none who does not believe that the safest and soundest course is to go on the assumption that the illness is "real" until proved otherwise. Non-medical people perhaps fail to realize that the physician quite frequently spots a fabricated story, but at the same time is equally aware of the panic and anxiety behind the need to fabricate it.

Concepts of malingering in general have recently undergone quite an overhauling. In World War II, Army physicians recognized that soldiers desperate enough to malinger were in all probability ill and it was recommended that the need for their malingering be explored. The drug addict's desperate need should perhaps be handled in the same way.

The law stipulates that all prison inmates be allowed to report for sick call. In a prison-hospital such as Lexington, this is a trying time for both physicians and patients. The patients have spent long hours devising schemes for getting drugs or medications of any kind. They are responding to the accumulated tension of being trapped and therefore unable to appease their need for drugs. All these elements together naturally make their frustration tolerance very low indeed. They perceive any slight injury as a major catastrophe and each one feels with his whole body and mind that he not only deserves but needs drugs. Other patients reporting for sick call are observed over perhaps a week to be working themselves into a hysterical panic, with concomitant physical reactions. Such patients may be given medication to insure a few nights' sleep, with the clear understanding that this is a temporary measure. Unquestionably, giving them temporary medication stimulates their attempts to obtain more medication. This delicate situation involves balance and timing: the administration of a small amount of medication to reduce their mounting hysteria and yet not enough, or of long enough duration, to stimulate their needs to a point beyond their control. It may also be said that no medical person can ever be truly convinced beyond doubt that the drug addict's appeal is based on pure deception.

I once treated a 27 year old nurse, who complained of a recurrent cystitis, for which she had previously consulted one of my colleagues whose name she had obtained from a training hospital. She told him that she had had a kidney removed; a large scar on her back bore witness to this fact. She appeared to be in acute distress, with temperature, pallor, tenderness in the lumbar region. The physician did a urinalysis in his office and discovered crenated red blood cells which, together with other findings revealed in a thorough examination, seemed to substantiate her story. She stated that she was working as a nurse, and as she seemed to be quite intelligent, there was no reason for the physician to suspect anything out of the way.

She requested morphine but instead was given a prescription for Demerol, which she said she could administer herself. She phoned the next day to say that she was allergic to Demerol and asked him to leave a prescription for Dilaudid at the drugstore. He did so, and within twenty-four hours he called her to check on the condition. To his surprise, there was no such telephone number as the one she had given. When she again phoned for medication, the physician suggested that she first come in for another examination and mentioned the desirability of hospitalization. She made some excuse and he never heard from her again. He then realized that she was probably an addict, but he was puzzled about the appearance of crenated red blood cells in the urine.

Several months later this woman was arrested for stealing drugs from a hospital. She was sent to a prison-hospital and, by coincidence, I recognized her from my colleague's description of the diagnostic picture and her clever ruses to obtain drugs. A little probing cleared up the mystery of the crenated red blood cells: before she consulted a physician she put a small pencil up into her urethra, causing bleeding into the bladder.

This woman's entire period of hospitalization was characterized by self-inflicted injuries in an effort to obtain drugs while surgical repairs were being made. She swallowed, among other things, a wristwatch, glass, broken pieces of silverware, stones and safety pins. In a continuous state of anxiety when off drugs, she could not work consistently. One night I was summoned to her room and found her sweating profusely, with dilated pupils and a low-grade temperature. She complained of a severe pain in her lumbar region. Examination of the urine showed crenated red blood cells. Despite the patient's previous history of feigning a kidney condition, she was given the benefit of the doubt and Demerol was prescribed until a medical work-up could be completed.

She continued to complain of severe pain and on the following day a flat plate of the abdomen revealed an opaque area in the region of the left ureter. On a tip from the technician, I examined the patient before she had her next x-ray and found on her back a flat wad of chewing gum mixed with some calcium-like material which would simulate a stone on the x-ray plate. The Demerol was stopped but she continued to require medication from time to time and, in fact, demanded as much attention as ten other patients.

There was no doubt about this woman's difficult medical history and even in a purely custodial arrangement she could not cope with her problems. As a matter of fact, she hanged herself while doing a short term in a house of detention where she was forcibly and suddenly withdrawn from drugs. In my opinion, this particular patient needed drugs to handle her emotional and psychic turmoil just as the diabetic needs insulin in order to function well. Fortunately this type of case is a rarity.

PHYSICAL EXAMINATION

The general physical appearance of the drug addict reflects the degree of comfort guaranteed him by his supply of drugs. If he is experiencing slight withdrawal symptoms, he will appear acutely ill: pale of face, with damp and clammy skin and trembling hands. His pupils may be pinpointed or dilated, or they may show a fluctuating reaction to light, as well as difficulty in accommodation. He will in all likelihood be very restless during the history taking. There may be evidences of vitamin deficiency such as blepharitis or chilitis. Physical examination will reveal a general malnutrition and air of neglect. The general body and muscle tone will probably be poor. He may have an astonishing amount of dental decay, be sloppy in dress and careless in personal hygiene.

The most conclusive evidence of present or past addiction is the presence of numerous small black and blue marks over the areas used for subcutaneous injections, usually the upper or lower arm or the thigh. A recent needle mark is indicated by a small scab. A patient who has been injecting into the "main line" will have characteristic vein markings. Veins used repeatedly become sclerosed and appear dark blue. They are so prominently outlined that the person's whole superficial venous system can be traced. The veins most commonly used are those in the antecubital fossa, on the back of the hand, in the ankles and feet, and in the groin. Female patients have been known to inject drugs into the veins of the breast. It has already been mentioned that addicts who are sufficiently desperate will inject any kind of drug they can lay their hands on, and frequently the physician sees an addict whose whole body is pitted from scars of old abscesses caused by injecting barbiturates and opiates. Addicts become very skilled at locating veins and can even use those along the sides of the fingers. Men who obtain contraband drugs while imprisoned will use the veins of the penis, if necessary, to escape detection.

It is impossible to diagnose drug addiction from the many other signs, including general malnutrition, because they vary in degree from patient to patient. To repeat, the addict's appearance and general physical condition reflect his ease or difficulty in obtaining drugs. If he has a steady source, and can afford the tariff, he may eat well, sleep well, and have a bodily appearance indistinguishable in all outward aspects from the non-addicted individual.

Laboratory examination may reveal an anemia resulting from insufficient food intake. This is no chemical test to indicate to the physician—or the law enforcement agency—how recently a drug which is found in the body may have been taken; nor is there any laboratory test, as we have already said, which will either prove or disprove addiction to drugs.

BEHAVIOR

The drug addict's behavior, too, is conditioned by his drug supply. He may appear nervous or excessively cautious. If he has recently taken a shot, he may stare off into space during the interview and become easily distracted. Often an addict will close his eyes rather slowly and then open them as if with effort, giving the impression of drowsiness or sleepiness.

When talking with known or suspected addicts, I have found that using their own argot for the various products and activities of the drug world usually helps to establish a good rapport. These terms are freely used by practically all addicts throughout the country and are therefore readily understood. The use of such expressions as "goof ball" or "yellow jacket" for sleeping pills, "main liner" for a shot directly into the vein, "speedball" for a mixture of opiates, often breaks the ice and may elicit a revealing response (see Appendix, page 171).

HISTORY TAKING

The history taking is much simplified if the addict admits his illness. Indeed, his history is otherwise bound to be full of distortions and outright false statements. A review of bodily symptoms will turn up certain ones which indicate active addiction. Addicts share in common various digestive disturbances, complaining of a lack of appetite, a tightness or "butterflies" in the stomach. Women patients will give a history of amenorrhea and men will complain of a loss of the power of erection. With amazing consistency they insist that when on drugs they never have colds, whereas they are dogged by all sorts of minor ailments when they are off drugs.

ESTABLISHING THE DIAGNOSIS

To diagnose an active addiction when the patient is determined to conceal everything possible is a real problem for the physician. Proof will rest on the patient's exhibition of withdrawal symptoms when removed from any drug source—a step which of necessity requires hospitalization. And even then the withdrawal symptoms may be mild enough to be mistaken for a common cold (which would disappear with a shot of morphine).

There is, however, a method of showing the presence or absence of an active addiction which can be used in the physician's office. It is based on the pharmacological action of N-allyl-normorphine or Nalline. Active drug addicts given a sufficient amount of this drug show typical withdrawal symptoms within twenty minutes. For a relatively mild habit, as much as ten to fourteen milligrams may be required, but in the presence of a strong habit, two to five milligrams will precipitate all symptoms. Nalline must be used very cautiously inasmuch as large doses may produce severe withdrawal symptoms which cannot be controlled with morphine for at least two and possibly as long as four hours after injection. Since there is no immediate antidote, it is wise to begin with a small dosage and wait for thirty minutes before increasing it if there is no effect. The ensuing refractory period must be borne in mind when using this most valuable diagnostic aid. Perhaps in time the findings obtained through using this drug will, as they should, be accepted as legal proof of the presence or absence of addiction.

LABORATORY IDENTIFICATION OF DRUGS

The identification of drugs, frequently required to clear up medical or legal problems, taxes the technician's skill. Few laboratories in the United States are equipped to give an identification accurate enough to stand up in the courts. It is, of course, far simpler to identify opiate drugs in powder form than to identify them from the often minute traces found in the body. The U. S. Public Health Service Hospital laboratory at Lexington employs the Staas-Otto extraction method for detecting opiates in the body fluids. This test will reveal opiates twenty-four hours after they have been taken into the body. In fact, for several weeks traces of morphine will appear from time to time in the urine of a strongly addicted individual. An excellent account of the chemical procedures used in identifying drugs is given in Maurer and Vogel's work.[4]

Most of the opium derivatives as well as the synthetic narcotics can now be identified from the urine. The test for each opiate, with the single exception of codeine, rests upon converting it into its original morphine form, which is then tested. Heroin and Dilaudid are also tested by the morphine content in the urine. Opiate determination by means of these elaborate tests takes from eight to twelve hours and requires a skilled laboratory technician. Although tests for barbiturates are considerably simpler, they too require special apparatus and materials in skilled hands.

Because test results are used mainly to substantiate clinical findings, witnesses must be present every step of the way—collection of the specimens, sealing of the bottles, opening of the bottles, and so on. Evidence is not conclusive if there is a reasonable doubt of accuracy, such as an opportunity for substituting a specimen, for instance, or improperly sterilized glassware. For this reason it is wisest to use Federal and state laboratories with the proper know-now and facilities as well as a staff especially trained in this particular type of testing.

TREATMENT

As we have seen, prescribing narcotics to alleviate a drug addict's withdrawal symptoms is, at present, not considered legitimate medical practice. The physician is faced with a dilemma: he cannot treat this obviously ill person and, in the vast majority of cities, including some large metropolitan centers, he can refer the patient neither to a local hospital nor in fact to any other place, except expensive private hospitals, for treatment. If the addict evidences his willingness to undergo hospitalization at Lexington or Fort Worth, the physician may get permission from the local narcotics bureau to give him drugs until he is admitted. The fact that a person without funds for travel fare and like expenses may find it virtually impossible to go to Kentucky or Texas for treatment, or that this type of prison-hospital may not be the most desirable place for him, is not taken into consideration. Futhermore, if the 60,000 addicts in the United States—considered by authorities to be a conservative estimate—were to request this sole legal form of treatment, the 2,000 beds available at Lexington and Fort Worth combined would hardly meet the demand.

Most discouraging of all, if an addict is not yet ready to go off drugs, he must continue to rely on the underworld-dominated black market.

These facts point to the crying need for wider medical recourse for the drug addict, victim of an illness which is perhaps even more devastating than alcoholism but which has elicited very little sympathetic response.

REFERENCES

1. Wikler, A. et al.: Precipitation of "abstinence syndromes" by single doses of N-allynormorphine in addicts. Fed. Proc. *11:* 402, 1952.

2. Oberst, F. W.: The determination of morphine in the urine of morphine addicts. Journal Lab. & Clin. Med. *24:* 318, 1938.

3. Turfitt, G. E.: The Identification of the clinically-important barbiturates. Quart. J. Pharm. & Pharmacol., *21:* 1-9, 1948.

4. Maurer, D. W., and Vogel, V. H.: Narcotics and Narcotic Addiction. Springfield, Charles C Thomas, 1954.

VII. Withdrawal Treatment

THE WITHDRAWAL TREATMENT of the addict requires of the physician not only medical knowledge but, equally as important, a familiarity with the details of custodial care. The simple fact is that the finest medical treatment can be totally invalidated if the basic and ever-present custodial needs of the patient are neglected.

It must be remembered at all times that the addict who has decided on treatment is in a progressively acute anxiety state, a condition that will be alleviated only with the completion of his treatment. The fact that he previously has been through one or more withdrawal treatments has not conditioned him to handle this anxiety. And the physician may conclude with some certainty that the longer the patient has been on drugs without interruption, the more alarm he will generate before and during the withdrawal process.

It follows, then, that the degree of friendliness and warmth which the physician is able to give to the patient will to a great extent determine the ease of the process for both. This does not mean that the physician should in any way give false reassurance, for it is impossible to go off drugs without acute discomfort (as the addict well knows). The patient's cooperation is obtained by explaining to him in minute detail just what symptoms he may expect and when he may expect them; by assuring him that the acute suffering will be over in from three to six days, and that in the meantime everything possible, within the limits of the treatment plan, will be done to allay his discomfort. Above all it must be made clear to the patient that he will be given adequate medication for sleep each night.

At some point early in the treatment it is inevitable that the patient will become frightened by his own decision to go

114   THE DRUG ADDICT AS A PATIENT

off drugs. At this juncture the physician will have to be extremely patient, retracing and reaffirming the thinking that went into the patient's original resolution. However, the addict's fright will often become so pronounced that no amount of reassurance will reduce it. This is the time to provide custodial care.

The physician must be constantly alerted from this point on, because no matter how sincere is the addict's resolution to go off drugs, he is apt to try to conceal them on his person and to make deals with nurses, attendants, members of his family and others to furnish him with drugs. *This can be considered normal behavior for an addict about to undergo or undergoing withdrawal treatment.* All those concerned with the treatment of the addict should be warned that such attempts will be made, but the physician should view them as signs of a very deep disturbance, and not as signs pointing to a poor prognosis.

TREATMENT AT HOME

Many patients will try to persuade the physician that they can undergo treatment at home, but this is rarely successful. As desperately anxious as the addict's relatives are to have him off drugs, they usually cannot withstand his suffering and pleading during withdrawal. Almost inevitably the patient manages to get hold of drugs and returns to his former state of addiction. In one instance I was confident that withdrawal could be accomplished at home because the addict's father was a physician. I had hoped that his professional experiences as well as the bitter experiences he had had with his son would have toughened him sufficiently to resist the boy's agonized pleading. It soon became apparent that the patient was not going off drugs although the father denied that he was furnishing them. Finally the patient confessed his father's complicity. This father, a normally honest physician, identified with his addicted son to the extent that he lied to me just as his son had done.

But though hospital care is always preferable, there are cases where home treatment can be made to work.[1] Before it is attempted, the physician must be certain that he can rely on the family or nurse to cooperate fully in administering the prescribed sedation and to hold out firmly against the patient's pleas.

HOSPITALS

Although the available hospitals are many and varied, the physician will have to take into consideration the financial situation of the patient and his family. In the majority of cases the family's resources have already been exhausted and public hospitals must be used. The three types of institutions to be considered are: Federal hospitals, of which there are two maintained by the United States Public Health Service (Lexington, Kentucky and Fort Worth, Texas); general hospitals; and private sanitoria.

General hospitals will, as a rule, accept drug addicts and are quite capable of fulfilling the custodial requirements. The many private sanitoria range from psychiatric hospitals to hospitals specializing in the treatment of alcoholism and drug addiction. Since 1952 the city hospitals in New York, and recently those in other large cities, have opened their doors to drug addicts for treatment. However, it is still possible to find hospitals operated by city funds for the general welfare refusing to treat patients with the medical illness of drug addiction. It is hoped that physicians will make their voices heard in the plea to reverse this policy wherever it is encountered.

Application for admission to the two Federal hospitals can be made directly to the medical officer in charge. As a rule, patients are admitted to these institutions with little or no waiting. However, there are no facilities for treating women patients at Fort Worth. At Federal hospitals, patients who are unable to pay are treated free of charge; others pay five dollars per day.

Reasonable and available though they are, certain factors detract from the desirability of such institutions as Lexington and Fort Worth hospitals. They are filled by referrals from the courts, and as a result most of the patients have a long record of arrests for petty criminal activities and recidivism. Since most of the addicts are there against their will, this leaves them with but one goal: to get out and return to drugs. It is highly likely that a patient's withdrawal treatment in one of these institutions will increase his underworld connections by scores.

In recent years, the Federal hospitals have attempted to segregate first admission and voluntary patients from the recidivists who comprise the majority. This has been done to provide an environment more conducive to changing the patients' attitudes about drugs. But segregation per se cannot accomplish positive results; these hospitals are badly understaffed and therefore cannot give the patients either intensive personal attention during withdrawal or psychiatric care which is so necessary afterward.

My opinion, borne out by experience, is that any treatment center which brings active drug addicts together in large numbers is bound to fail in its purpose. Whenever possible I would recommend treatment of the addict either in a general or a psychiatric hospital.

In this context I should like to refer to treatment of the adolescent addict, who is generally believed to present an entirely different problem from the adult addict. This seems to me to be erroneous, for his youth in no way makes his habit less serious than that of his older counterpart. If anything, the adolescent is less motivated to go off drugs than the older addict whose years of imprisonment may figure in his motivation toward that end. A nineteen-year-old drug addict once said to me of an older addict who had tried to counsel him, *"He* can talk. He's had years of it. I'm supposed to get off and I've only been on drugs two years. I feel as if I'm being gypped!"

ESTIMATING THE HABIT

It is impossible to estimate with any degree of accuracy the amount of drugs a patient has been taking. Fortunately, such information is not important, for as little as 1/4 grain or 1/2 grain at most of morphine four times a day will prevent severe withdrawal symptoms regardless of the degree of habituation. It is nevertheless important for the physician to show interest and concern over the amount of drugs the patient *says* he has been taking. In his anxiety state when facing withdrawal he will probably lie about his previous intake in an effort to persuade the physician to give him more drugs. In many cases the patient may believe his habit is very strong, but inasmuch as drugs on the black market are greatly cut, the amount he thinks he has been taking might actually prove to be fatal.

A safe rule is to give no more than 1/2 grain of morphine four times a day or 20 milligrams of methadone four times a day.

THE ADDICT IN CUSTODY

Immediately on the patient's admission to the hospital, the physician's custodial knowledge must be put into practice. The patient should immediately undress, have a bath and put on regulation hospital wearing apparel. Many narcotics are water soluble, so the patient's clothing should be laundered before being returned to him in case drugs have been concealed. The next step is a thorough physical examination, which may disclose drugs hidden in any of the body orifices, including the rectum or the vagina. A common practice is for drug addicts to swallow encapsulated narcotics which they retrieve later from their stools. A nurse warned beforehand to watch out for any patient who is unduly concerned with his stools may prevent this.

The patient should be informed before he is admitted that he will not be allowed any personal belongings, mail or visitors for the first few days. The addict's family or well-intentioned friends often send narcotics or sleeping pills in letters or food packages. I recall the case of a physician who was being withdrawn from drugs. Although he complained of great distress, his appetite remained hearty. I suspected a slip-up in custodial arrangements. A check revealed that his office nurse, his only visitor, was supplying him with drugs. The patient had convinced her that I was giving him too severe a treatment and that furnishing him with some drugs would not retard the treatment but merely make it more bearable. Taken in by this tale, she had brought him cocaine in nose drops, despite the fact that she knew he would lose his medical license if he did not go off drugs immediately and permanently.

The patient's pleas during his acute period of suffering are so heartbreaking that even nurses and attendants are likely to look on the physician as an ogre. In fact, everyone on the scene will feel a desire to relieve the patient's misery.

The ultimate success of withdrawal treatment depends largely upon preventing the patient from obtaining drugs. It cannot be emphasized too strongly that he is not apt to be cooperative in this respect. Consequently, the physician must be sure to choose a hospital or sanitorium that can furnish the proper custodial care to enable the patient to free himself of drugs.

Frequent and thorough physical examinations are required during the course of withdrawal, for the patient may simulate a medical illness with uncanny accuracy. Diagnosis of this type of malingering is often very difficult, requiring both laboratory and diagnostic acumen. Among the chief symptoms drug addicts simulate are attacks of precordial pain radiating down the left arm, resembling angina or coronary heart disease, and back pain in the region of the kidney resembling a kidney stone attack. Further subterfuges used by the addict are covered in Chapter VI, *Clinical Diagnosis.*

METHODS OF TREATMENT

There are three methods used in withdrawal treatment of drug addiction: (1) abrupt withdrawal or "cold turkey"; (2) abrupt withdrawal with substitute therapy such as insulin; (3) gradual withdrawal using morphine or methadone.

Abrupt ("Cold Turkey") Withdrawal

In the method popularly known as "cold turkey," no narcotics are given and symptomatic treatment alone is extended to the patient. This is considered, and with ample reason, to be an inhuman form of treatment. It is involuntarily experienced by many drug addicts in various penal institutions, and other addicts who have heard its horrors related are thereafter generally afraid to volunteer for any type of treatment. The only time the "cold turkey" method should be used is when it has been directly requested by the patient.[1] Several of my patients have made this request, convinced that the agony, though almost unbearable, is not as prolonged as in the other two methods. Even though I doubt this statement, I generally accede to the patient's wishes unless the method is medically contraindicated.

Abrupt Withdrawal with Substitute Therapy

The second method consists of abrupt withdrawal accompanied by supportive treatment with the use of such drugs as hyoscine, insulin, calcium gluconate, or by prolonged narcosis or electroshock.[3] It has now been established that these supportive forms of treatment cause more difficulties and hazards than the withdrawal itself.[4] With insulin therapy, for example, the symptoms of hypoglycemia so closely resemble withdrawal symptoms as to defy differentiation.

In the early days of ACTH and cortisone there was considerable publicity to the effect that these adjuncts would cure drug addiction. Research has disproved this optimistic claim; in fact, instead of helping in any way they appear to aggravate the withdrawal syndrome.[5]

The few preliminary reports on the use of chlorpromazine (Thorazine) in withdrawal treatment[6, 7] are so favorable as to merit discussion here.

Chlorpromazine is administered intravenously in 50 mg. doses and intramuscularly in 100 mg. doses following the abrupt withdrawal of morphine. The doses are repeated at four-hour intervals, and after two days the drug is given orally. It has been found that the patients sleep for as long as twelve hours at a stretch. To avoid postural hypotension they must remain in bed but are roused for intravenous feedings. After two or three days of almost solid sleep the dosage is reduced. According to reports,[6] the patients are then very cooperative and, interestingly enough, they do not usually demand narcotics. The drug seems to allay their intense anxiety symptoms, always present in withdrawal.

In one series of reported cases,[7] sleep during withdrawal was insured by the addition of barbiturates. Smaller dosages of chlorpromazine and up to 700 mg. of barbiturates were administered daily to induce sleep lasting from sixteen to twenty-one hours.

Although it may well be that these early successes will be borne out by more thorough long-term research, which is now going on at Lexington, recommendation of this withdrawal treatment is withheld until such research is completed.

The method of withdrawal which has thus far proved most successful is that employing either morphine or methadone. In general these drugs are adequate substitutes for whatever drug or combination of drugs the patient has been taking. When morphine is substituted, the withdrawal symptoms will be more severe than with methadone but the patient will be relatively comfortable within a week. With methadone, his withdrawal symptoms will be much less severe but he may feel shaky for as long as a month afterward. By and large the morphine withdrawal treatment seems more satisfactory, although both will be outlined in detail.

An important contraindication to the use of morphine or methadone is a primary addiction to Demerol or to codeine. In these cases it would be unwise to introduce them to the stronger narcotic. Withdrawal can be accomplished by using the drug to which they have been addicted.

Withdrawal with Morphine[8]

The patient is put on 1/4 grain (0.015 gram) morphine four times a day. The dose must be administered on a rigid schedule: twenty minutes before each meal and at bedtime. This insures the maximum comfort during eating and sleeping. The most severe withdrawal symptoms occur within the first seventy-two hours. If too severe, the morning and evening shots may be increased to 1/2 grain (0.030 gram). All doses should be given hypodermically, preferably dissolved in thiamine hydrochloride. Oral sedatives should always be dissolved to prevent the patient from accumulating them and taking them in one massive dose. After two days on 1/4 grain morphine q.i.d., the first change is to substitute 1/8 grain (0.007 gram) morphine for two of the daily dosages. The following day the patient can be given 1/8 grain four times a day and he is kept on this dosage for one or two days. The next change is to substitute two 1 grain codeine doses for two of the morphine, until codeine is being given for all four shots. Codeine is then reduced to 1/2 grain dosages and finally is alternated with thiamine. When the patient is receiving four doses of thiamine a day, the final step is to wean the patient from all hypodermics—by progressively eliminating them.

It will readily be seen that this is a modified rapid withdrawal method. If such a course seems desirable the patient can, of course, be stabilized for a longer period at each dosage reduction.

Withdrawal with Methadone

The methadone withdrawal treatment consists of stabilizing the patient on morphine and then substituting methadone. With this substitution, the withdrawal symptoms are milder but longer lasting than with morphine. The most severe symptoms occur between the seventh and the ninth days.

The patient is placed on morphine for two or three days as in the morphine withdrawal plan; for example 1/4 grain four times a day. Then methadone is substituted for two of the daily dosages and the following day methadone is used exclusively four times a day. After a week on the same amount, the dosage is reduced and within three or four days it can be eliminated entirely.

A calculation of the amount of methadone to replace the stabilizing dosage of morphine is as follows: for 30 mg. (1/2 grain) of morphine substitute 10 mg. of methadone. Thus a patient who has been stabilized on 1/2 grain of morphine (0.030 grams) four times a day can easily be held on 10 mg. of methadone four time a day.

The physician and nurses can avoid a great deal of dissension and overt anxiety on the part of the patient by refusing to divulge the drug or the dosage given.

TREATMENT OF WITHDRAWAL SYMPTOMS

Withdrawal symptoms vary in intensity with individaul patients; they may be mild, moderate, marked or severe. However, even the most severe symptoms (rising temperature and blood pressure, vomiting, diarrhea with rapid loss of weight) must be considered in relation to the patient's total picture. Vomiting and diarrhea are alarming only when they reach excessive proportions, causing dehydration. The extremely rare fatalities during treatment are due mainly to withdrawing drugs too abruptly or too rapidly. The method advocated here should preclude any serious results. Constant supervision by the nurse will catch in time any such serious symptoms as rapid pulse or shallow irregular breathing.

An experienced nurse is of inestimable help to the physician. If inexperienced, the nurse in charge must be given specific instructions and told what to expect in terms of the patient's behavior. The nurse must watch the collection of all specimens and supervise the temperature taking. Drug addicts know how to raise a thermometer reading, prick a finger to put blood in their urine, or cause themselves to vomit. They will often swallow blood in sufficient amounts to produce a positive test in their stools in order to simulate a bleeding ulcer. The nurse's report, of decisive importance in evaluating the severity of withdrawal symptoms, should include a three-times-a-day temperature check, a daily check on weight, blood pressure, respiration and pulse rate, food and fluid intake, and consistency of the stools.

The clinical manifestations of withdrawal are lacrimation, dilation of the pupils, rhinorrhea, yawning, goose flesh, sneezing and excessive perspiration. Most patients lose their taste for food and therefore lose weight during the treatment. The two factors in a rapid decrease in weight are a lack of caloric intake and a loss of fluids by diarrhea and vomiting. The nurse should immediately report a rise in temperature or in blood pressure, either of which may indicate too rapid a withdrawal. All patients will suffer from extreme restlessness and insomnia. A serious dehydration may occur within a relatively short period. A patient who is vomiting and suffering from diarrhea should be given saline infusions to bring the total daily intake of fluids to a minimum of 3000 cc. Although excessive vomiting can be a very depleting symptom, it occasionally occurs as a hysterical conversion symptom, in which case withdrawal can proceed. Vomiting of this type invariably ceases with the completion of withdrawal treatment. Severe muscular aches and pains always accompany withdrawal, and the patient's restlessness is in part an effort to handle this pain. Hot baths or flow tubs give relief and should be prescribed several times a day.

Helpful symptomatic treatment includes tincture of belladonna and atropine to relieve the nausea which keeps many patients from eating. Bismuth will help control diarrhea, althought the patient is sure to insist that only paregoric will do the trick. One-half grain of phenobarbital can be given three times daily to handle excessive restlessness. Since most patients are markedly undernourished, multiple vitamins should be prescribed. Sedation at night must be adequate to insure rest; an additional dosage left with the nurse will take care of insufficiencies on this score. I have found that most addicts require a minimum of 3 grains of Nembutal during this period with an occasional repeat of 1 1/2 grains if they are not getting more than five hours sleep a night.

The physician should not become alarmed at the variety and intensity of the patient's subjective feelings. Almost invariably his one goal is to obtain more drugs and he will use any ruse to accomplish it. His subjective complaints will probably continue right up to the last day of withdrawal. But although a drug addict's pathetic state can well cause the physician more worry than a patient with an acute abdomen, before increasing the dosage at the insistent behest of the patient, the physician should exhaust all the diagnostic facilities and, with the nurse, make a careful study of the daily notes and charts.

The length of hospitalization will vary with the individual. For an initial withdrawal, i.e., the first time the patient has been off drugs since becoming addicted, the maximum period of three to four months is recommended. For the relapse of a patient who has been readdicted only for a short time and is involved in a total treatment plan (described in Chapter VIII, *Rehabilitation*), two to three weeks may be sufficient. It may be considered more important for such a patient to keep his job than to have a long hospitalization which would jeopardize it. Certainly any patient should be hospitalized long enough

to receive the medical or dental care he needs in order to re-
gain his appetite and weight and to get into the habit of sleeping well without medication.

One of the major purposes of hopitalizing a patient for
three months for an initial withdrawal is to give him the experience of coping with a "yen"–his term for an overwhelming
craving for drugs. This "yen" is frequently accompanied by subjective feelings that resemble withdrawal symptoms, and even
simulate them physically. It constitutes a real danger for the
unhospitalized patient since he is quite unable to use any kind
of logical reasoning to control it. Life itself seems unimportant
to him compared to satisfying this craving at the moment it
occurs. The hospitalized patient finds that the acute craving
passes within half an hour to three hours—a revelation to many
drug addicts who have not heretofore withstood the craving
long enough to find out that it will leave.

Another advantage to this prolonged hospitalization is
that it allows the addict to become reacquainted with his own
body sensations, and to learn not to be afraid of them. The
normal morning fatigue experienced by everyone is regarded
with alarm by the addict. The slightest muscular ache or pain
brings on an attack of anxiety; an occasional bout with indiges-
tion means he is dying of cancer of the stomach, etc. It will
thus be seen that a long hospital stay will provide the opportunity for some much needed re-education.

CONTRAINDICATIONS TO WITHDRAWAL

Withdrawal of drugs is perfectly safe, from the health
standpoint, with very few exceptions. The presence of another
illness besides addiction is no deterrent. Similarly, the age of a
patient who is otherwise in good health does not constitute any
hazard. In fact, it is often gratifying to see the numerous symptoms associated with a concomitant illness disappear, one by
one, when the patient is off drugs.

In the notable medical exceptions—cardiac cases, acute infections and surgical procedures—certain measures take priority
over the launching of withdrawal.

Cardiac cases require a complete medical work-up and digitalization prior to withdrawal. During this period the cardiac addict should be maintained on a routine which includes sufficient morphine to preclude any acute physical distress. In all probability one-half grain of morphine four times a day will accomplish this purpose. Once digitalization is completed, withdrawal treatment can be started. The withdrawal treatment outlined above should be slowed down so that it extends over a period of approximately one month additional by stabilizing the patient for three or four days after each reduction in dosage.

Addicts suffering from acute infections or requiring emergency operative procedures should be maintained on either one-quarter or one-half a grain of morphine four times a day until the treatment or surgery is completed, after which time withdrawal can be instituted.

Even in chronic disease cases or terminal illnesses, patients do considerably better if the narcotic dosage is kept at a minimum. With larger amounts, the secondary toxic results of the narcotic—constipation, apathy, etc.—are likely to aggravate the chronic illness.

CONCOMITANT BARBITURATE ADDICTION

The likelihood of barbiturate addiction must always be considered when treating drug addicts. Frequently they may be taking as many as forty grains of barbiturates daily in addition to other drugs.

It is preferable to withdraw the addict from morphine before attempting barbiturate withdrawal.[8] During morphine withdrawal the patient should be stabilized on barbiturates. Usually three grains of one of the shorter-acting barbiturates (pentobarbital or secobarbital) given orally four times a day is sufficient to maintain the patient in barbiturate balance. Sufficient barbiturates should be used to produce a moderately intoxicating effect.

Approximately one week after the patient has recovered from the withdrawal of morphine, barbiturate withdrawal can be started. It must be remembered that barbiturate withdrawal is much more dangerous than morphine withdrawal[7] since there is *no substitute drug* that can be used to allay the symptoms.

Barbiturate withdrawal symptoms range from extreme weakness to tonic-clonic convulsions, visual and auditory hallucinations.

The addict who is abruptly withdrawn from barbiturates first experiences extreme weakness, accompanied by gross tremors of the hands and facial muscles. The systolic blood pressure and pulse are elevated, as is the non-protein nitrogen content of the blood. Disorientation, with loss of recent memory, occurs after two days of withdrawal. Convulsions and psychosis usually occur within the first week, although the patient may suffer blackout spells as late as two weeks after withdrawal is completed.

Treatment for barbiturate addiction consists of stabilizing the patient on a moderately intoxicating dosage of a barbiturate as mentioned above and gradually reducing the dosage over a period of two or three weeks, or even a month in cases of a very strong addiction.

Intravenous Sodium Amytal should be constantly on hand in the ward for emergency use in case of convulsions or psychosis brought on by too rapid withdrawal.

LEAVING THE HOSPITAL

Preparations for the patient's rehabilitation should begin as soon as he is off drugs. If a member of Narcotics Anonymous, a psychiatrist, a group counselor, a rabbi or a priest is to be included in the treatment plan following the patient's release from the hospital, contact should be made in advance, so that he will have some place to go and a sense of being wanted—an alternative to seeking out his old drug addict friends. In the event that a staff psychiatrist is willing to treat the patient further after he is released, individual interviews can be started while he is still in the hospital. The gap between the carefully regulated hospital treatment and the problems which the drug addict must face when on his own should be reduced to a minimum; a firm continuity must be established if the over-all treatment is to be successful.

Of the patients who leave the hospital toward the end of withdrawal or immediately following it, many are merely interested in reducing their intake of drugs and have no intention of embarking on a full rehabilitation treatment. The physician should not react adversely when he becomes aware of this intention. He should rather give the addict the feeling that if and when he may decide to make the effort to stay off drugs, the physician will always be ready to help.

When the patient is discharged from the hospital, the physician may wish to prescribe a tension-relieving drug. This has always presented a problem. Heretofore, the best available drug to relieve tension and induce sleep has been one of the barbiturates, but physicians are mindful of the ever-present danger of the patient's substituting barbiturates for their former drug of choice and thus becoming addicted anew.

Chlorpromazine (Thorazine), a drug recently developed in France, is now being extensively used for this and many other purposes. Discharged patients are given it in a dosage of 25 mg. three or four times a day. Some physicians allow them to take one 25 mg. tablet whenever they feel tense, regardless of the total daily intake. Although the results of this relatively new drug are not yet fully known, it seems to keep some of the post-addict's tension well below the point where a relapse to drugs constitutes his sole relief.

Of equal importance is the physician's continuing contact with the patient, maintained ostensibly for the practical purpose of renewing prescriptions and watching the blood count as required in this therapy. The physician's role as helper and friend is thus reaffirmed. The addict appreciates these attentions and is particularly grateful that someone in authority is trying to relieve the terrible tensions behind his addiction.

REFERENCES

1. Wikler, A.: Drug addiction. In Tice's Practise of Medicine. Hagerstown, Prior, 1953.
2. Isbell, H.: Meeting a growing menace—drug addiction. Merck Report. July, 1951.

3. Howe, H. S. and Morris, L. S.: Treatment of withdrawal symptoms of persons addicted to narcotic drugs. Welfare and Health Council of New York City, 1954.
4. Maurer, D. W., and Vogel, V. H.: Narcotics and Narcotic Addiction. Springfield, C. C Thomas, 1954.
5. Isbell, H., and Fraser, H. F.: Relationship of the pituitary-adrenal system to the morphine abstinence syndrome. Tffects of cortisone and ACTH. (To be published.)
6. Friedgood, C. E., and Ripstein, C. B.: Use of chlorpromazine in the withdrawal of addicting drugs. New England J. Med. 252: 230-233, 1955.
7. Aivazian, G. H.: Chlorpromazine in the withdrawal of habit forming drugs in addicts. Dis. Nerv. Syst. 16: 57-50, 1955.
8. Nyswander, M.: Withdrawal treatment of drug addiction. New England J. Med. 242: 128-120, 1950.

VIII. Rehabilitation

THE MOST CRUCIAL STAGE in the treatment of a drug addict begins at the moment he is released from the hospital where he has been withdrawn from drugs and has spent from six weeks to four months in a drug-free environment. His return to social and work life depends to a great extent on beginning this part of the treatment at once.

The complete rehabilitation of the drug addict may extend from one to three years, during which time the physician must be prepared to be taxed to the utmost. However, if he knows ahead of time what to expect and how to handle each problem as it arises, the task, though difficult, is far from impossible.

As we have seen, it is simple enough to withdraw a drug addict from drugs. Unfortunately, too much emphasis has been placed on the importance of this part of the therapy. Removing a patient from drugs and leaving him in a drug-free environment even for four months is not enough. A majority of the patients I have seen give a history of relapsing to the use of drugs within one to twenty-four hours upon release from an institution. The withdrawal of drugs, while of course the basic factor, is by no means the *only* factor in the total treatment of the drug addict.

To be successful the treatment planned for a drug addict must take in every area of his life. In fact it requires the complete resources of the community in much the same way as the paraplegic's treatment and rehabilitation require wide resources of help. Though this may seem an insuperable task, actually the physician's greatest responsibility in the treatment plan is to be an authoritative and sympathetic "crutch" and to make contacts for the patient with the various community agencies that may be able to help him.

Many workers in this field believe that a psychiatrist should be the supervising physician in such a total rehabilitation plan, because they doubt that a person can voluntarily stay off drugs without insight into the emotional problems which caused him to go on drugs in the first place.[1] However, the available statistics on addicts who have stopped taking drugs do not bear out this conviction. On the contrary, they show very clearly that the decision must have been made without the help of a psychiatrist.[2] In the long run, as with alcoholism, the patient's inner decision to stay off drugs determines the cure. A large area for future work should be centered around the determination of the usefulness of psychiatric techniques in aiding the addict to make this decision, and reinforcing it, once made.

THE PHYSICIAN'S ROLE

The physician is in a peculiarly favorable position to help the drug addict. Because of his scientific knowledge and the respect which he commands in the community, his overtures in the way of interest and understanding will probably constitute the first motivation for the drug addict to get well. The addict has undoubtedly exhausted the patience of his family as well as his "respectable" friends and they have long since ceased to trust him or try to understand him. As we have seen, drug addicts seek out others of their kind primarily because they understand each other's weaknesses and struggles. The physician who shows that he realizes the drug addict's suffering during withdrawal, who seems to appreciate the courage required to make one of the toughest fights known to mankind, has already helped to supply the most important need in the life situation of a drug addict: to be understood.

One may well ask: what precisely is the role of the physician in the treatment of the drug addict? If the addict is not on drugs and is not sick, what can the physician do for him? How can the physician influence his life pattern? The self attitude initially presented to the physician shows little that will motivate him toward any course other than a return to drugs— his one sure pleasure.

The physician's first efforts should be directed toward establishing himself as a warm, friendly authority. His position in the patient's life should be a unique one, neither duplicating the parents' anxiety and criticism nor the law's harshness. The physician must establish that he sincerely understands the patient's struggles and difficulties, while making clear that his only personal interest in the patient's addiction is a *shared* concern. The very first appointment may lay the groundwork for motivating the addict toward a decision which will probably be many months away; namely, to stay off drugs. The physician's simple offer to help the patient do what he wishes to do—resist drugs—will prove to be an unbelievably strong influence in this direction. Many experts feel that instilling fear or using threats will have the same effect. But any student of human nature knows that such measures play only a small and temporary role in any real cure. This is the role of the law and it should not be employed by the physician.

The physician's sincerity is further shown by a willingness to discuss all phases of the drug addict's immediate life situation. His source of livelihood, an adequate history of his work problems, his immediate plans for work, his long term goals and his feelings about them—all are important in establishing the proper rapport. The social life of the drug addict must also be probed. How is he going to spend his evenings? Is his environment pleasant and satisfying to him or is it an unhappy one? Is his family setting conducive to good adjustment? Are his friends for the most part drug addicts? Does he feel he can see them without succumbing? Questioning the patient about these areas will reveal to the physician where temptation may be lurking.

For example, if the patient is returning to his old neighborhood where former addict friends may live in the same building, the physician should ask him to be frank about his ability to handle this situation, while showing that he fully appreciates its difficulties. The patient may express a desire to help in finding a new environment, saying, "I don't have any friends except drug addicts. I know this is bad, but what am I going to do?" At this crucial point the physician must be prepared to help bring about the necessary changes which the patient is not able to do alone. He literally needs to be helped as if he were a child. He can avail himself of help but cannot yet initiate it.

The physician will therefore have to make appointments with the appropriate agencies or organizations that can fill the patient's needs. The patient feels the physician's strength in handling the community, which he fears, and this in turn gives him strength. With his fear of society and his fear that he will fail, he tends to view every situation with hopelessness. He anticipates failure and invites it by not trying. Thus it is important that he have a kindly authority to guide him, particularly at the beginning, and to do certain things for him which he cannot do unaided.

In addition to conveying his interest in every aspect of the patient's life, his sincere desire to see the patient happy, the physician should give assurance that he will be available when the patient's temptations become too difficult to be coped with on his own. Many a patient has withstood the urge to take the first shot by calling his physician, by feeling free to talk to him. The success of treatment thus depends, all along the way, on the establishment of this unique relationship between patient and physician.

The physician's role—to be at all times authoritative and understanding without adopting the patient's feeling of hopelessness—is a very difficult one. Upon his first relapse to drugs, the patient will try to convince the physician that he is hopelessly and permanently addicted. The physician's refusal to accept this self-made diagnosis may be the only strength the patient has to go on for some time.

The second important function of the physician in the treatment of the drug addict is to plan and to make available to him such help as he may need. To this end, the physician must have knowledge of many sources of help that can be called into play when the occasion arises.

It is essential that the physician have a reliable and cooperative hospital where he is known and where he can be in constant touch with the patient in case hospitalization is necessary. All social agencies which can aid the patient in matters pertaining to employment and housing, as well as the various community groups which may meet other of his specific needs, must be explored against the time when a referral would be beneficial. A psychiatrist or psychiatric clinic whose fees are within the patient's means should be contacted. Every addict needs a strong, healthy group to replace the drug addict group he is trying to break away from. The physician should be familiar with functioning groups in the community that will accept the patient immediately—for example, Narcotics Anonymous, which now has branches in many of the larger cities of the United States. This group will be discussed at length later. Group counseling and group psychotherapy are also available in most large cities today.

Lastly, the physician must honestly assess his progress toward establishing himself as the over-all authority in the patient's life. If he has not succeeded in this respect he must be prepared to suggest another authority with whom the patient may be able to establish a closer relationship.

Religious advisors sometimes play a very important role, even on occasion superseding the physician.[3] The drug addict's guilt is so overwhelming that he cannot believe the physician's interest in him is genuine and he may be better able to accept such interest from a priest or a rabbi. Two adolescent addicts known to me were befriended by the rabbi associated with a reformatory where they served a year's term. The rabbi, who was extremely sensitive to adolescent needs, never told them what to do or what not to do, but merely discussed life problems in a general way and told them of some of his own inadequacies and anxieties. This marked the first time they had ever heard a respected man admit to sharing their own feelings. With a close bond established, the rabbi was able to persuade them to join Narcotics Anonymous upon their release. Their contact with him has been maintained over the intervening two-year period and his interest undoubtedly still figures in their motivation for staying off drugs.

Any physician who undertakes certain phases of the treatment of drug addicts will require a knowledge of adjunctive therapies which will be described in detail later in this chapter.

DIAGNOSIS OF NEEDS

Diagnosis in the context of a treatment plan is primarily in terms of the addict's social adjustment. The neurotic and psychopathic personalities among drug addicts have similar characteristics. The psychotic drug addict may resemble the others in certain aspects, with the addition of a severe mental illness.

From the total mass of information yielded by patients, two grossly different life stories will emerge. One group will present a picture of irregular work, an inability to hold jobs, a lack of skilled training, limited education, a history of frequent arrests for burglary, assault or the like. These patients are usually the psychopaths. Their daydreams and wishes fail to reveal any well defined, socially acceptable goal. When questioned, they usually reply that they want to be big shots, own a Cadillac, be rich. One such patient who declared that he wantèd to be a musician had not the remotest idea of the training necessary in pursuing a musical career. As adolescents, these patients were frequently members of gangs. The majority of the patients at Lexington fall into this category. It is unfortunate that public opinion and attitudes toward treatment, as well as existing laws, have been based primarily on the psychopathic addict. There is, however, growing evidence to support a more optimistic view of the treatment of psychopaths; their response to Narcotics Anonymous, for instance, has been remarkably good.

A typical neurotic drug addict's history will often reveal a middle or upper middle class background; parents who are skilled workers or professional people; a high school or college education or, in the case of a school problem, obvious capabilities for such training. His aspirations, though perhaps unfulfilled, are apt to be specific. He may not have had any brush with the law, or if so it was a single episode. Although his work record is likely to be sporadic, this type of patient shows a desire to succeed in a socially acceptable position.

The psychotic patient, who presents an entirely different problem, requires supportive psychotherapy. The physician will immediately sense that this person has little ability to handle reality; a certain vagueness and illogicality provides the clue to his serious mental illness. If the physician is in doubt, he can arrange a psychiatric consultation in order to determine the exact nature and extent of the illness. On the whole, psychotic patients are best handled in a clinic setting, for their total helplessness requires a great deal of social service work.

CANCELLED APPOINTMENTS

In order to make the drug addict feel that there is one person in the world who will stick by him, the physician will have to schedule frequent and definite appointments and insist that they be kept. One of the problems for the physician is that contact as often as every other day, either by personal appointment or phone call, may be necessary to affirm his interest in the patient, and to provide a means of checking on the patient's progress in life adjustment. It may take some time for the addict to show enough aggression to make his own appointments, to feel "worthy," as it were, of making such a request.

It has been my experience that the drug addict never breaks an appointment unless he has relapsed to drugs, in which event he does not feel able to face anyone. Even more important is the fact that he feels the physician will like him and help him only as long as he is succeeding. This is characteristic, too, of his feelings about his boss and family. It explains his inability to ask anyone for help on a job. Instead he runs away, to avoid the harsh treatment he is sure will follow. If a good relationship has been established, the patient will respond to the physician's efforts to contact him and will return, ashamed and humiliated, to confess his "degraded" state of addiction. In reassuring the patient, the physician should explain that a straight line to cure is no more to be expected in the treatment of drug addiction than in alcoholism. Victims of both are bound to stumble and fall on the way. Bolstered by the physician's determination to maintain close contact, he will feel a renewed effort to fight this disease and will sincerely assure the physician that he wants to go off drugs and will do it by himself.

During a relapse the physician will have to assume the full responsibility for making appointments. After a week or so he may find a propitious time to suggest that since it is admittedly very difficult to take oneself off drugs the patient might like to avail himself of a hospital. This idea will very likely meet with immediate resistance: he doesn't feel that he is really addicted to that extent; he would like to cling to the belief that he can take himself off drugs. This is mere self-deception —a postponement to permit him to stay on drugs a little longer. However, after a short period of frequent visits, daily if possible, the patient will probably ask for hospitalization.

The chagrin and humiliation which the patient feels at his first relapse are multiplied a hundredfold at his second relapse—in my opinion the most dangerous time in his entire treatment, for he then loses faith not only in himself but also in the physician's ability to help him further. If the kind and considerate aid of the physician, interested agencies, his boss and others, has failed to keep him off drugs, he feels he must indeed be a hopeless victim. He is reluctant to go on involving other people in what seems a losing battle. These self-defeating attitudes are also part of his unconscious psychology: to perpetuate the idea of himself as a drug addict. This double battle becomes very discouraging and it is necessary to explain and re-explain that as he is growing stronger he is pushing his desire for drugs into a corner and in turn the desire is pushing back even more strongly. Caught in between, he will seem in his own eyes more helplessly victimized by drugs than before he started treatment.

TREATMENT OF RELAPSES

Relapses to drugs are handled as they occur and are not to be viewed with alarm. Relapses lasting for a week to a month or two do not require the full scale withdrawal treatment recommended initially. Indeed, hospitalization for one to three weeks may suffice.

The standard treatment drug addicts receive in a hospital which is not geared to their needs frequently serves to break down the little determination they have built up prior to entry.

One such experience I had with a 22 year old drug addict, father of a child, was most disheartening. His approach to therapy was unquestionably sincere. In three months he had taken himself off drugs and returned to high school to obtain his equivalency certificate, while working in the daytime. As was to be expected, with the first difficulty in his work he sought old friends and relapsed to drugs. Addiction occurred quickly and his habit built up rapidly. At the end of one week of daily sessions he expressed a desire to be hospitalized in order to get off drugs as quickly as possible. He was admitted to a city hospital where the physician in charge of his ward gave him a long moral lecture, revoked his wife's visiting privileges and threatened to commit him to a state hospital. This physician also informed his family that any doctor treating a drug addict in an ambulatory state was stealing his money.

The young man became thoroughly frightened. His relationship with me was impaired and although his family would not consent to having him committed, they refused to let him continue his psychotherapy. The total effect was a weakening of his resolution to stay off drugs and he relapsed soon after leaving the hospital. This particular failure was totally unnecessary—the result of mismanagement. It is well to forewarn patients that they might be subjected to similar experiences, or more constructively, to advise family and hospital personnel of the adverse effects of such negativistic attitudes.

Hospitalization for relapses should not be prolonged, because the longer a drug addict withdraws from society the greater his fears become. The best antidote for these fears is found in his daily successful experiences in society, at work and with friends.

Like the inveterate smoker who says, "There's nothing to cutting out tobacco; I ought to know—I've done it fifty times," the drug addict who has been off drugs at some time during his period of addiction is in an advantageous position: he is better able to handle some of his anticipatory anxieties about repeating the process. Even so, all addicts will need considerable reassurance when facing this ordeal.

According to the literature on drug addiction it is axio-
matic that an addict must be hopitalized in order to be taken
off drugs. On the whole this is true, especially for one who has
never been off drugs since he became habituated. The drug
addict's acceptance of hospitalization is always a good prognos-
tic sign. But if in the course of treatment the physician feels
confident of his good faith and intentions it may be more
strengthening for the patient to try to cure himself.[4] I have
seen patients even in the first year of therapy voluntarily go
through the "cold turkey" method or take themselves off drugs
with the help of three methadone pills daily and chloral hydrate as a night sedative.

It cannot be overstressed that the real aim of a rehabilitation program is to help the patient master his *desire* for drugs.
If an addict is kept behind bars, the hospital or institution becomes the *depriver*. True rehabilitation helps him to summon
the strength to deprive *himself*—a decision he will ultimately
have to face. Drugs will always be available, just as alcohol is
always available to the alcoholic. Inner motivation cannot be
strengthened by continually taking drugs away from the patient. He must at some point push them away. And in the latter
stages of therapy, his once valid desire to be hospitalized for
relapses must be challenged. It can be pointed out to the patient
that he can do the same thing without the institution's help;
that his attitude of helplessness is prolonging his illness; that
as long as he clings to this pretense he will not be able to
overcome his passivity sufficiently to make the great fight to
say "no."

Several types of hospitals may be used to treat the relapse
of drug addicts. The major difficulty is to find one that will
admit them. The best solution—a private hospital with facilities for psychiatric patients—is usually very costly. Recently,
city hospitals in large cities throughout the country have revised their policy and are accepting drug addicts for withdrawal treatment. An explanation to the admitting physician
that the addict is in treatment will usually bring about cooperation. However, the patient should be prepared for a certain amount of cruel derision and hostility due to the great

public pressure and moral indignation which have been built
up around this illness.

If the patient's relapse has been not longer than a week or
two in duration, two or three hypodermic injections of 1/4
grain morphine spaced over one twelve-hour period will usually
suffice to take care of the relapse. He should have the security
of knowing that he will receive adequate sedation. A drug addict can sweat it out during the daytime if he can look forward
to some relief at night.

In the event that the patient cannot afford hospitalization
and other community facilities are lacking, it is possible, though
difficult, for a member of the family or a trained nurse to take
over the job. The patient must be willing to let such a person
be his "jailer." This chosen aide should in no case administer
any narcotics but he can give the night sedatives quite satisfactorily.

AMBULATORY HOSPITALIZATION

The method which I call ambulatory hospitalization is an
excellent one for rehabilitation for the neurotic patient. Unfortunately its cost is prohibitive except to a few, but in my
opinion the great success of this technique warrants a thorough
investigation with a view to its widespread use for the treatment of drug addicts. Ambulatory hospitalization is offered in
many private psychiatric hospitals whose names can be obtained
by contacting the local county medical association or department of hospitals, or the American Psychiatric Association.

Under this method, the hospital becomes the patient's
"home" throughout his whole rehabilitation treatment. It may
also be the place where he is initially taken off drugs, in which
case he may remain there as long as a year. During this time
the patient has a daily one-hour interview with the trained
psychiatrist to whom he is assigned. Social workers and educational counselors work on other aspects of his problems.

When both the patient and his psychiatrist feel confident
that he is ready, he makes his first step into the outer world
by leaving the hospital grounds, perhaps to see a movie. The
length of his leave is gradually increased until he may be able

to resume his schooling, go home for weekends, and so forth, always returning to his hospital "home." As he further builds up his strength, he may take a job—still under the protective influence of the hospital and its staff. An important corollary of this treatment is that he is forced to make friends of other patients. Thus he has the backing of a group and of authorities whom he views in a friendly light, not with the same fears and antagonisms he held for teachers, bosses and persons in authority in his own family.

A striking success of this method is demonstrated in the case of an 18 year old drug addict. The son of successful professional parents, he had been arrested twice and at the time of my first interview with him was on probation. He had been on drugs for four years, had stolen and pawned his family's possessions, and his parents were ready to wash their hands of him. Psychiatric help was their last desperate hope.

The boy—tall, handsome and intelligent—expressed a sincere desire to stay off drugs. His self-esteem was extremely low. Despite his obvious intelligence he had tremendous feelings of inadequacy in comparing himself to his father and other members of the family. He had no confidence that he could pass the simplest courses as a freshman in college and suggested that if I really wanted to help him I could write his psychology papers. He talked very freely, although somewhat glibly, about himself. He felt devastated by the position he was in and understood, as do all drug addicts, that his family's distrust was the result of his own repeated lies.

After a few months his family began to report finding bottle caps and bent spoons in his room; then clothing and other articles disappeared. The patient was not divulging anything about these happenings. After one of our sessions he spent an unusually long time in the bathroom. The sounds of preparing a shot were unmistakable. I asked him about this and he readily admitted that it was true; he had been back on drugs for two weeks. He asked to be hospitalized and was sent to a private hospital where he remained for a total of eight months.

During this time he ran away twice and was brought back by his family. His daily sessions with the hospital psychiatrist continued throughout his stay. He gradually integrated with the group and participated in activities involving the patients. He was given limited visiting privileges, fell in love with a girl and had his first satisfactory love affair. By the end of his hospitalization he had been off drugs for five months, had resumed college and was making excellent grades. In the intervening four years he has not relapsed. For over a year after his dismissal he continued therapy under the hospital psychiatrist, with whom he had formed an excellent relationship.

The ambulatory hospital method may not be in use in all local psychiatric hospitals, in which case it will be necessary for the physician to explain it and work out the details with the staff. The usual treatment for drug addicts is to keep them in the hospital with no outside privileges until the day they are released.

PSYCHIATRIC CARE

Although drug addicts, like other patients with medical illnesses, have attending or causative emotional problems, they may neither need nor want psychiatric help. Yet the literature on the treatment of drug addiction, after the physician was no longer allowed to handle addicts, reveals that it has been largely left in the hands of the psychiatrist. Early studies were carried out from a psychiatric point of view, in line with the belief that a solution to the problem lay in the drug addict's personality. However, one cannot say that all cures depend upon the patient's gaining insight into his own personality problems. After all, hospitals such as Lexington, which give little or no psychiatric help, also turn out a certain percentage of cured addicts.

Nevertheless, it is certainly true that the psychiatrist has much to contribute to a complete understanding of the drug addict's behavior, and it is also true that his cure involves the mobilization of an emotional determinant in his personality. In the treatment of an alcoholic it is not necessary to close down all the bars or to threaten the hapless victim with imprisonment; he either makes the decision to stay off or he doesn't. And so it is with the drug addict. The most important factor in his decision to reject drugs is his ability to build up other real satisfactions[4]; he will then not wish to jeopardize them by relapsing to drugs. Many patients will require a psychiatrist's guidance in finding the necessary satisfactions in human relationships, work, marriage, sex, and so forth.

Patients who do not respond favorably to the physician's suggestion of individual psychotherapy will often accept a less direct form of psychiatric treatment, such as group therapy, which may be just as beneficial.[1] Unfortunately, the psychiatrist's techniques are pretty much limited to those patients who really want treatment. For example, a 22 year old male drug addict consulted me, not because of his addiction but because of his relationship with his wife. "I know I should love her for all the help she's given me," he said, "but I just don't. When I'm with her I'm always thinking about other girls. The same thing happened with a girl I was going with before I got married, only I broke off with her." It was apparent that without working through the emotional problems presented by his marriage, this patient would have a slim chance of remaining off drugs. Helping to resolve this kind of emotional block to the patient's happiness is the province of the psychiatrist.

Psychiatric treatment will vary with the patient, the psychiatrist and the clinic. A minimum of one regular weekly interview should be scheduled and, in addition, the psychiatrist may arrange an experience in group psychotherapy.

Psychiatric care at low cost is difficult to find anywhere, although the larger cities are more likely to have private low-cost clinics and psychiatric training institutions. The cost varies from as little as two dollars a visit, charged by many hospitals, up to ten dollars or more.

Unfortunately, psychiatrists are not immune to the country-wide wave of moral indignation aroused by narcotic users and they, too, may reveal a lack of sympathy and empathy by lecturing the patient at length. The patient should understand that he is not committed to continue with a psychiatrist he doesn't like; the person in authority should make an effort to find him another therapist who inspires confidence.

The average psychiatrist's schedule is not flexible enough to allow him enough time to arrange for adjunctive therapies, and for this reason many physicians favor referral to a psychiatric clinic where social workers, psychologists and counselors can arrange for those services.

COMMUNITY GROUPS

The drug addict's need to become part of a group immediately upon completing his hospitalization for initial withdrawal, cannot be overemphasized. The physician or any other interested person in charge throughout this period can smooth the way by arranging for a group leader to visit the patient in the hospital.

Although they are frequently so described, addicts are not solitary people; they have many contacts and derive great support from their wide circle of addict friends.[5] The real friendships established are unfortunately destructive because they are based on the mutual supplying of drugs. However, the addict's need for a group is a positive asset which should be utilized. When the physician learns of the existing groups functioning in the community, he may then decide which will best fit the patient's needs and wishes or he may let the patient decide for himself.

Social workers are familiar with all of the local social agencies and are very helpful in making referrals to specific groups. Drug addicts by virtue of their associations have attained what seems to them a high degree of sophistication, and it would not be wise to refer a seventeen-year-old addict to a settlement house group of teen-agers whose major interest is baseball or basketball. Generally speaking, the 18 to 25 year old addict will be likely to feel more comfortable in an adult group.

Many agencies and hospitals have active groups meeting regularly in the evenings. They may be primarily social or oriented toward working out certain adult problems. Usually there are openings for new patients. The YMCA and the YMHA have group activities centered around "Y" social activities.

The increase in group therapy in metropolitan centers has opened up a large and invaluable field of help, as well as providing a ready made, non-addict group experience for the patient. The American Psychiatric Association will refer the physician to clinics, institutions, or private psychiatrists offering group psychotherapy. The fee for group therapy is of course considerably lower than for individual therapy.

Group psychotherapy has the distinct advantage of offering the patient a valuable life experience in a controlled situation. A group usually consists of eight or ten members who meet once or twice a week; their membership is constant and a group may remain in existence from one to four years. The group may be led by a social worker, a psychologist or a psychiatrist, either as part of his private practice or in connection with a hospital clinic. The individual fees range between two and five dollars. Essentially each is made up of people who discuss all their life problems and also their feelings about one another, in an effort to find out what factors contribute to their unnecessary tension. The thought of participating in such a group is perhaps frightening to the average person and doubly so to the drug addict, for he cannot imagine being accepted if his co-members were to know his real thoughts and feelings and what he has done. An addict requires preparation and reassurance before he will feel able to join such a group.

NARCOTICS ANONYMOUS

This organization was founded in 1948 by Danny Carlson, an ex-drug addict. Knowing how difficult it is for post-addicts to stay off drugs, he felt that they would be immeasurably helped by joining some group activity. His intuitive reasoning was that drug addicts would be most likely to gain support from ex-addicts—the only people, in their opinion, truly able to understand their frailties and their tremendous temptation to fall back to the habit of drugs. The organization, still in its infancy, is patterned on and functions very much like Alcoholics Anonymous. Financial problems from the start have cramped their program: outside support has been negligible and addicts themselves are not usually people of means. However, at present there are branches of this group in most large cities throughout the United States and Canada and they hold group meetings twice a week.

Mr. Carlson attempts to contact drug addicts while they are hospitalized for withdrawal or while they are still in reformatories or prisons. His warm interest and understanding form the patient's first bulwark against a future relapse. He is often there when the patient is released and escorts him to a group meeting which has been carefully selected with his best interests in mind. The whole group takes a lively interest in a new member, putting him at ease, urging him to obtain employment and giving him practical help toward that end.

In its early days Narcotics Anonymous was widely suspected of being merely a convenient blind—a place for addicts to meet and share information about drug sources. To counter this propaganda their meetings are frequently opened to physicians and other interested non-members. When a member relapses, the group effort is immediately directed toward getting him off drugs. Often their scanty funds are pooled to help send a member to Lexington or elsewhere for withdrawal treatment. Although members actively on drugs are not retained in the group, they are assured of acceptance once they are off drugs and, even more important, the group's interest does not lessen because they have relapsed. In these meetings, an individual often for the first time hears others discussing their temptations and problems. It is very enlightening for him to hear others using the same rationale he has used so frequently and thought was exclusive with him. Like the alcoholic, every drug addict feels that his problem is unique.

Narcotics Anonymous members are very active; a new member is assigned to the care of an older member, and whenever the going is rough he calls his patron, who usually insists that they meet to talk things over.

The group therapy method in a setting exclusively of ex-addicts is particularly effective for those addicts with a history of antisocial behavior. In general, the group's present membership is of a fairly limited educational and social level, and it does not offer much of a solution for the patient from a middle or upper middle class background. Branches in different cities will of course vary in this respect.

It is too bad that Narcotics Anonymous has had so little encouragement and backing from community leaders that it must struggle along with insufficient funds. The by-passing of this group is in all probability due to the deeply ingrained and widely held belief that drug addicts cannot get together for any constructive purposes.

NEW ENVIRONMENT

It is unfortunate, although perhaps necessary from the standpoint of administering a probation schedule, that a patient who is arrested must be returned to the place of his arrest. In fact he must remain within the city during his entire probation unless the officer in charge grants him special permission to leave. If a relative in a different city will assume responsibility and if a job the patient feels he would like is in the offing, a talk with his probation officer about the possibility of making a special plan may be worthwhile.

The addict is observed maintaining a kind of facade to impress his old friends. As a rule he displays an entirely different personality with them: he "talks tough," swaggers and has a general air of bravado. He tries to give them the impression that he is a fearless he-man. Appearing before them as a legitimately employed clerk, dutifully going to work in the morning and coming home at night, spending his evenings at the movies or going to dances, would lay him open to insufferable derision. One of my patients really needed eye correction, but none of his drug addict friends had ever seen him with glasses and he felt they would look on him as a sissy. He wore his glasses elsewhere but took them off when he went into his friends' neighborhoods. He took a big step forward when he was able to wear his glasses in their presence—symbolic of standing up to this group and defying them to tease him or decry his new-found values.

Anyone working with drug addicts quickly comes to realize how little encouragement and bolstering they need to break with old patterns which have at best given them only temporary and partial satisfaction.

The difficulty in long-term planning for drug addicts lies in their need to gratify each impulse at the moment.[4] As we have already noted, they want money and prestige immediately and without effort. One must point out that aside from the entertainment field, a spectacular rise is not the norm; that it is not a mark of inadequacy to have to plug for several years before attaining an adequate salary; that they are in the same boat with everybody else in this respect.

As the drug addict gains more confidence and loses some of his anxiety and tension, his pleasures will naturally increase. When his gratifications have increased to the extent that they constitute a positive force, the drug addict, like anyone else, will be reluctant to exchange the pleasures of reality for the certain destruction guaranteed by a return to drugs.

The final stage in the drug addict's treatment consists of breaking off his dependency relationship with the physician. It will gradually become apparent that the patient is working primarily for his own pleasure, not for the purpose of pleasing the physician by reporting his progress. One or the other of them will then undoubtedly terminate the visits. The physician, aware that a relapse can occur at any time throughout the patient's life, should always leave the door open in the event that further encouragement and help are needed.

It is safe to say that a patient who has actively worked on his life problems for three years under a physician's supervision has probably hurdled the major ones. Any future relapse which comes later on in his life should be relatively easily handled. Far from being a serious threat, it will mean little more than a couple of steps backward, quickly to be regained.

REFERENCES

1. McNickle, R. K.: Drug addiction. Editorial Research Reports. Washington D. C.
2. Vogel, V. H., Isbell, H., and Chapman, K. W.: Present status of narcotic addiction, J. A. M. A. *138:* 1019, 1948.
3. Adams, Walther, A.: Narcotic Drug Addiction and Out-Patient Treatment. Annual Report on the Activity of Medical Counseling Clinic of Provident Hospital. June, 1954.
4. Savitt, R. A.: Extramural psychoanalytic treatment of a case of narcotic addiction. J. Am. Psychoanalyt. A. *2:* 494-502, 1954.
5. Goldstein, Nathaniel L.: Narcotics. A report to the Legislature of State of New York; Legislative Document, 1952, No. 27.

IX. The British Approach

INTRODUCTION

THE ENGLISH EXPERIENCE with drug addiction has been dramatically different from that of America. Their maximum estimate of 500 addicts is startling in its smallness. Although their Dangerous Drug Act is similar to our Harrison Act, the interpretations and administration of their laws have resulted in the continued cooperation and interest of the physician in the treatment of drug addicts. Typical of this cooperation is a report from Detective Sergeant George Lyle of Scotland Yard,* stating that he found that "most doctors prescribing drugs were all right. The very few wrong ones are detected. We are fortunate in this country as there is little of the social evil of drug addiction." He thought that this was because "addicts are able to get their drugs from doctors and there is little traffic. Without traffic there is less danger of new people being drawn in." This working relationship between enforcement officers and physicians has been consistent, in England, over the decades (see Chapter I) and has resulted in keeping the problem of drug addiction in the hands of the physician.

The comparability of the English and American experience with drug addiction might be challenged; it could be pointed out, for example, that the English drug problem never equalled our own in degree or intensity; or again that a homogeneous population like that of England represents a far different series of problems than those found in the type of heterogeneous population found in the United States. However, even though direct comparisons of these two national experiences are not

---

*Lyle, George: Dangerous drug traffic in London. Brit. J. Addiction 50: 47-58, 1953.

valid on all levels, this chapter is included in the hope that we may profit by the examination of the methods used in a country which has successfuly dealt with the control and treatment of drug addiction; and that we may thus gain some perspective on our own attitudes which can help us formulate ideas specific to our needs.

A COMMENTARY ON THE MANAGEMENT AND TREATMENT OF DRUG ADDICTS IN THE UNITED KINGDOM

By JEFFREY BISHOP, M.B., B.S. (Lond.), M.R.C.S., L.R.C.P.*

General Remarks on the Law and the Problem

"In 1858, John Simon, first and greatest of a long line of men distinguished for their work in preventive medicine, reported to the Privy Council on the causes of 'infantine mortality in different districts in England,' and mentioned that 'infants who should be at the breast are improperly fed or starved, or have their cries of hunger and distress quieted by those various fatal opiates which are in such request at the centres of our manufacturing industry. . . . Women when remonstrated with on the subject of drugging their children with laudanum, say that they must keep their infants quiet, as their husbands and older children, who have to work during the day cannot do so if disturbed at night.' In one Birmingham factory, employing 150 women, it was said that ten out of every twelve children born to these women died within a few months of birth."[1]

In spite of this alarming report which was written nearly a hundred years ago, I do not think that drug addiction has ever been a real problem in this country. There is no doubt, however, that the use of substances which we now know to be drugs of addiction was common in England long before there

---

*Member of Council, Society for the Study of Addiction; Clinical Assistant, Department of Dermatology, St. Mary's Hospital, London; Part-time Medical Officer, Diabetic Department and Medical Out-Patient Department, The Royal Free Hospital, London.

existed any effective control over their use and in the pre and post 1914-18 war years drug addiction was on the increase. The first form of control in Great Britain was in relation to opium and cocaine and was brought about in 1916 when a measure, amending the Defence of the Realm Regulations of 1914, was proposed in an endeavour to prevent persons possessing, selling, giving or supplying such drugs to other than authorised persons, or otherwise than in accordance with their authority; records involving transactions in these drugs had to be maintained.

> "One day, soon after the first world war, Billy Carleton, the actress, was found dead in her flat. She had died of cocaine poisoning, the drug having been self-administered. This incidence is of importance in the history of cocaine: for the first time the public were made to realize that drug addiction had grown apace in London. Their support was thus assured for the passing of The Dangerous Drugs Act in 1920."[2]

This Act firmly places the responsibility for the management and treatment of the addict in the hands of the medical profession. It must be remembered that to be a drug addict has never been and is not now illegal in this country. The addict is committing an offence only if drugs found in his possession have been unlawfully obtained. He is regarded as a sick person in need of medical care and not as a criminal to be hounded by the Police.

Under the Act a doctor is authorised to possess, supply or prescribe dangerous drugs so far as is necessary for the practice of his profession. (Dentists, veterinary surgeons, pharmacists, nurses, etc., have a limited authority.) The Home Office have issued a Memorandum in which it is pointed out that a doctor may not have or use the drugs for any other purpose than that of ministering to the strictly medical needs of his patients. The continued supply of drugs to a patient, either direct or by prescription, solely for the gratification of addiction is not regarded as a medical need.[3] Anslinger has, I believe, mentioned this when comparing the regulations for controlling narcotics in the United States and Great Britain and it has also been quoted in support of a claim that the addict's relationship with the medical profession is essentially the same in the two countries.

In 1924 the Government appointed a committee under the chairmanship of Sir Humphrey Rolleston, Bart., K.C.B., M.D., P.R.C.P., "to consider and advise as to the circumstances, if any, in which the supply of morphine and heroin (including preparations containing morphine and heroin) to persons suffering from addiction to these drugs may be regarded as medically advisable. . . ."[4] At that time it appeared to the Home Office that ". . . in some instances, the drugs were being supplied and used in contravention of the intention of Parliament, namely, that the use of Dangerous Drugs should be confined to that which was necessary for medical treatment."[4] The Home Office took the view that they were reluctant to take proceedings against doctors for offences against the Dangerous Drugs Act until various doubtful points, which turned on questions of medical opinion, had been elucidated by a responsible body of medical men. Extracts from the conclusions arrived at by this committee and the advice which it gave to the Home Office are contained in the Memorandum to which I have already referred.

They are that morphine or heroin may properly be administered to addicts (a) under treatment by the gradual withdrawal method with a view to cure; (b) where it has been demonstrated, after a prolonged attempt at cure, that the use of the drug cannot safely be discontinued entirely on account of the severity of the withdrawal symptoms produced and (c) where it has been similarly demonstrated that the patient, while capable of leading a useful and relatively normal life when a certain minimum dose is regularly administered, becomes incapable of this when the drug is entirely discontinued.[4]

This is not to say that there are no circumstances in which a doctor may be prosecuted under the Act. Indeed during the year 1954 nine doctors were convicted for obtaining drugs for the gratification of their own addiction and nine persons were successfully prosecuted for failure to keep drugs in a locked receptacle or failure to maintain appropriate records.[5] Moreover, the Home Secretary has power, after the conviction of any doctor under the Act, to withdraw his authority to possess, prescribe or supply Dangerous Drugs. During 1954 this power was exercised in respect of three doctors.[5] A similar power may be exercised, without criminal proceedings, on the recommendation of a Medical Tribunal constituted in accordance with the Regulations under the Act. Such a Tribunal has, in fact, never been convened.

A prescription for any drug coming within the scope of the Dangerous Drugs Act must comply with various requirements. It must be dated, signed by the medical practitioner and must specify the name and address of the person for whose use the prescription is given; and it must specify the total amount of drugs to be supplied. Doctors must also keep a Dangerous Drugs Register in which is entered particulars of drugs obtained and supplied. No entry in the Register need be made when the drug is administered by the doctor or under his personal supervision.

Physicians

Cases of drug addiction are not compulsorily notifiable to the Home Office and a doctor is not required to obtain permission before attempting to treat an addict. However, a patient who is obtaining his drug from more than one doctor is committing an offence under the D.D.A. and it does help the Home Office to detect these cases if doctors inform them of the names of addicts in their care. There is no such thing as a Home Office or state registered addict, and an addict who is known to the Home Office is not in any way privileged.

Regional medical officers of the Ministry of Health who are appointed inspectors under the D.D.A. have power to inspect doctor's records of Dangerous Drugs and they are also available to give advice on cases of addiction. If a physician does not inform the Home Office when he sees an addict for the first time he will, sooner or later, be visited by the Regional Medical Officer and enquiries will be made as a result of the quantity of drugs he is using. It is in this way that doctors who are themselves addicts are detected. The physician would not, of course, reveal the name of his patient and the nature of his complaint to anyone without his patient's full knowledge and consent. This applies to a patient who is an addict just as much as to a patient suffering from any other disease or illness. However, he can make it a condition of his treating the addict that he be allowed to inform the Home Office of his patient's name and the drug to which he is addicted.

A medical practitioner who has had his authority to possess, prescribe or supply dangerous drugs withdrawn (following conviction of an offence under the D.D.A.) may continue to practise in any branch of his profession. If a patient of his requires a Dangerous Drug he must get a colleague to supply or prescribe it. There is certainly no intimidation of physicians by the Police or Home Office in this country—either with regard to drug addiction or anything else. There is a very real spirit of co-operation between the medical profession and Government and Police Authorities which has helped a great deal to keep this country free from organised drug trafficking.

Treatment

"There is of course no compulsory treatment of addicts in the United Kingdom and there are no State institutions specialising in problems of addiction. Treatment is left to the discretion of the doctor in charge of the case, and there are a number of public hospitals where addicts can be treated and several private nursing homes dealing exclusively with drug addicts and alcoholics."[6]

The attitude of a physician when confronted by an addict is to ask him if he really wants to be cured. If he says he does (and the physician believes him) then he is told that he can be helped if he is prepared to co-operate. Because we have so few addicts, only a handful of doctors have any experience of treating them. Most general practitioners would refer the patient for consultant opinion—probably a psychiatric opinion. However, there are a few physicians who, though not consultants in general medicine or psychiatry, are true specialists in that they have made a special study of the treatment of all forms of addiction. Even they have relatively limited experience in the field of addiction to drugs—most of their time being spent treating the alcoholic. The management of each particular addict

is left entirely to the physician in charge of the case. It follows
from this that each specialist has his own methods.

"I have never known a morphia taker accept treatment unless I
could promise that he should have a gradual tailing off of his
morphine intake. . . . In my early treatment of morphine addiction
I was content with simply detoxicating my patients. I cut down
the drug while giving intramuscular injections of apomorphine
three or four-hourly. I gave half a gramme of Soneryl Sodium each
night. All the more unpleasant symptoms (of withdrawal) were
removed and after fourteen days the patient could be discharged,
sleeping normally without artificial help. I was content with that.
A man taking 20 grains of heroin a day (equivalent to 60 grains
of morphine) was twice cut down to nothing in this way in under
a fortnight. Such people usually relapse in under six months and
require, and often receive, further treatment. I have treated
another patient taking 5 grains of morphia a day by giving
apomorphine by mouth for four weeks, and it helped him cut
it down and out, but he suffered a good deal. . . . I have not
treated any pethidine or marihuana addicts, nor a cocaine addict,
except two who were also addicted to morphine. They said they
lost the need for cocaine when they lost it for morphine, but I
was not able to follow up these cases."[7]

Dent has since treated a few cases of morphine addiction
by the same method he uses for the alcoholic, namely with
alcohol and apomorphine. He is emphatic that the success of
his treatment does not depend on any conditioned reflex or
aversion. He says "apomorphine not only takes away the necessity for alcohol but also for barbiturates, the necessity for morphine, heroin and sometimes the necessity for suicide."[8] He
insists on his patients being admitted to a nursing home for
the treatment and he promises the addict that he will give him
his drug as often as he asks for it, but in return he must promise
not to ask unless he really needs it. He has sometimes found
difficulty in inducing patients to take alcohol during treatment.
"Some morphine takers will say they have never sunk so low
as to take alcohol, just like the alcoholic patients who are proud
that they have never taken drugs."[8]

Some psychiatrists favour abrupt withdrawal of the drug with the administration of apomorphine, continuous narcosis or cortisone to mitigate to a greater or lesser extent the more severe forms of withdrawal symptoms. They follow this with simple psychotherapy and rehabilitation to life without the drug. Others taper off the drug and accompany this with longer or shorter forms of psychotherapy (e.g., psycho-analysis). Out patient treatment is generally thought to be impracticable and the stay in hospital or nursing home usually needs to be from a couple of weeks to a month or more.

There is often a delay of a few days or even longer after the addict is seen in the out-patient department until a bed in the hospital becomes vacant. (This bed shortage for non-acute admissions is a fairly common occurence here and is in the main due to shortage of nurses.) If this is so, the addict is instructed to attend the Casualty or Out-Patient department of the hospital, three or four times per day if necessary, in order to receive injections of his drug from the Casualty physician in doses stipulated by, and under the orders of, the physician in charge of the case. Any general practitioner may, if he wishes, treat the addict without reference to a psychiatrist or anyone else.

If the addict is treated under the ordinary conditions of practise and not in a hospital or nursing home, the doctor's aim will be either to get the addict off the drug altogether by gradual withdrawal or to reduce the dose to the absolute minimum. Under these circumstances where a continued supply will be given to the addict the Rolleston Committee[4] suggested that the patient should be seen at intervals of not less frequently than once a week. Moreover, the Committee expressed the view that as the decision to continue supplying the addict with his drug indefinitely is a serious one, the doctor would be well advised to obtain a second opinion.

Addicts sometimes voluntarily seek treatment from a particular physician; it may be that he goes to the doctor on the recommendation of another addict who has been cured by him. In this way a few physicians have become well known to the medical profession (and to addicts) as being willing and able to treat drug addiction with some measure of success. They thus tend to see more drug addicts than their fellow physicians.

One such doctor has recently told me that he has no difficulty in recognising the true addict. The way in which he gives his history, the clarity with which he describes withdrawal symptoms, puncture marks in the skin and thrombosed ante-cubital veins from the hypodermic needle all enable him to make his diagnosis with certainty. Often he can spot the addict as soon as he walks into his consulting room.

If the physician decides that the patient is not an addict but is pretending to be one in order to obtain drugs (i.e., a pedlar hoping to get a continuous supply of a drug) which he could subsequently sell, the physician would telephone Scotland Yard.

A close and honest relationship between addict and doctor is often difficult to establish, though this may not be true in the case of the better educated man or woman who realises the terrible dangers of continuing the addiction, and who is desperately anxious to be cured. No statistically significant analysis has been made of the number of addicts cured. Each individual physician sees too few cases to enable any worth while conclusions to be drawn. The following figures published by one institution where drug addicts are cared for may be of interest[9]:

Total number of patients treated.... 16
Cured.... 5
Uncured.... 8
Here on Staff.... 2
In a Home.... 1

The word "cured" means that patients are known to have been off drugs for periods of time ranging from 2 to 6 years.

The Police do, from time to time, raid dance halls, opium dens, etc., and arrest anyone found to be in possession of drugs *unlawfully* (as instanced in Det. Sgt. Lyle's paper read before the Society for the Study of Addiction in January 1953). Such person who has in some way contravened the Dangerous Drugs Act may be sent to prison. If he is an addict he will probably be taken off his drug straight away without tapering the dose. Prison doctors say they do not see the classical withdrawal symptoms described by others. It is thought that the classical "cold turkey" has two factors: the physiological and the functional. In prison, where the addict knows he will get no more of the drug, the functional element is eliminated and withdrawal reactions are less severe. This is not to say that the addict sweating out his "cold turkey" is consciously malingering but rather that he has a true hysterical overlay to the symptoms he exhibits. The prison doctor will, of course, administer drugs to those in his care if he feels they are necessary. Barbiturates or paraldehyde are sometimes substituted to tide the patient over the acute stage of withdrawal.

The Addict

Spencer Paterson[10] has classified addicts as follows:

(1) Iatrogenic; where the patient has been given opiates for chronic or recurrent pain.
(2) Unstable, tense individuals who have access to opiates (physicians, nurses, pharmacists, veterinary surgeons, etc.).
(3) Those in the entertainment world, whether artistes or pleasure seekers, who are likely to encounter traffickers.

The first group may be subdivided into (a) those patients suffering from some condition in which the possibility of cure is remote (e.g., inoperable cancer). Clearly, the establishment of a craving in such a patient is unimportant when compared with the seriousness of the disease. Increasing doses of the drug may be necessary and are fully justified if the patient thereby receives a measure of comfort unobtainable by any other means. (b) Patients suffering from organic disease but in which the necessity for powerful pain relieving drugs is expected to be of more or less temporary duration (e.g., renal colic). The Rolleston Committee reminded doctors that they would be wise, in this type of case, to substitute other drugs for morphine and heroin and to withdraw the drug as soon as the necessity for its administration has ceased. If an addiction forming drug must be given, the patient should not know its name. Hypodermic administration of the drug by the patient to himself is strongly deprecated.

The second group is self-explanatory and on the whole these addicts respond well to treatment.

The third group is the one which presents the most problems. Addicts in this group are often coloured dance band players but may also be white English men and women. These are the adolescents who frequent the cheap dance halls. They smoke a "reefer" in an attempt to show off in a dare-devil spirit or because they have been told it will make them more "sexy." (There is some evidence that marihuana lessens inhibitions, though long continued use of heroin weakens sexual desire.) Or a girl may be encouraged to take drugs in order to gain a hold over her and force her into prostitution.

Why doesn't every addict go to a physician for his supplies? The answer is that physicians do not *supply* drugs; they try to *cure* the addict. An addict who does not want to be cured or helped to cut down his dose, will therefore rely on illicit sources of supply. The very few who are being supplied by a pedlar either do not know that they can be helped by a doctor or are too frightened to seek advice.

If an addict is brought before the courts for being in possession of drugs *unlawfully,* the magistrate may put him on probation *provided he accepts medical treatment.* In this instance alone is the addict, under pressure of the law, required to do as the physician says. It is a condition of his probation that he receives medical treatment.

Social Attitudes and Statistics

Juvenile deliquency certainly showed a rise during the post-war years, and although there has also been a rise in the number of adolescents prosecuted for offences concerning marihuana I do not think the two are connected in any very significant way.

The Home Office arrive at the number of "known addicts" on information they receive from doctors, as explained in the introductory section. There are almost certainly more addicts than are included in these figures. How many more it is very difficult to state. Any figure would be only a guess, but there is no doubt that the number of unknown addicts must be very small indeed and of virtually no significance. My guess would be a total of approximately 400 addicts (known and unknown) and this includes people addicted to manufactured drugs and marihuana.

Generally speaking, I feel that to say "addicts make addicts" is untrue. Very few addicts influence others to start the habit. Their reaction to a request for a taste of the drug is usually to warn of its dangers and to point out what harm it had done to them.

The following are extracts from the British Government Report to the United Nations for the year 1954[5]:

The total number of known addicts was 317 (men 148; women 169). Among these were 69 doctors (3 of them female), 2 dentists and 1 pharmacist. (The estimated population of the United Kingdom at mid-year, 1954, was 50,784,600.)

No evidence of organised illicit traffic in manufactured drugs in the United Kingdom has come to light, nor has there been any case in which a person addicted to such drugs has been found to have obtained regular supplies from illicit sources. As in previous years a small number of addicts obtained supplies unlawfully from medical sources, e.g., by forged prescriptions and prescriptions from more than one doctor. The majority of persons addicted to manufactured drugs are over 30 years of age.

The use of cannabis is largely confined to persons of African, Asiatic or West Indian origin of between 20 and 40 years of age.

With three exceptions, all persons convicted of offences related to opium were of Chinese origin and in the majority of cases were over 35 years of age.

During 1954, morphine was used, either alone or in combination with other drugs, by approximately 65 per cent of the known addicts. The corresponding figures for heroin and pethidine were 17 per cent and 16 per cent, respectively.

With two exceptions all persons known to be addicted to manufactured drugs were resident in the United Kingdom. A large proportion of those using opium were transient seamen; so were a number of cannabis offenders.

Illicit traffic in the United Kingdom continues to be small. Traffic in opium has for some years been declining, and is largely confined to persons of Chinese origin. Seizures of cannabis in 1954 showed a marked increase. Illicit production of manufactured 'drugs and traffic in drugs illicitly produced is unknown. Such illicit traffic as exists is in drugs obtained by diversion from lawful sources (e.g., through medical prescription and very occasional thefts) and is not organised.

In 1954, 219 persons were convicted of offences relating to dangerous drugs. Of these, 28 were in respect of offences involving opium, 144 in respect of offences involving cannabis and 47 in respect of offences involving manufactured drugs.

Sentences of imprisonment in respect of opium offences ranged from 28 days to 6 months and fines from £2 to £115 (U. S. $5.60–$305).

Penalties imposed for the unlawful possession of cannabis ranged from 1 day to 3 years imprisonment and fines from £1 to £125 (U. S. $2.80–$350).

For offences involving manufactured drugs, sentences of imprisonment ranged from 6 to 12 months and fines from £3 to £100 (U. S. $8.40–$280).

The increase in the number of seizures involving cannabis and in the number of convictions of offences relating to this drug reflects, to some extent, increased vigilence on the part of H. M. Customs and the Police but it is thought that there has been some increase in the traffic itself.

There is no reliable information as to the price of drugs sold illicitly.

Summary

1. The position of the drug addict was drastically altered by the passage of the Dangerous Drugs Act. It meant that he could no longer buy his drug at the chemist shop without a doctor's prescription.

2. The effect of this was to bring the addict into contact with his doctor, who tried to cure or at least to help him.

3. Doctors may only supply or prescribe dangerous drugs for their patients when a real medical need for the drug exists; but the Home Office recognises that to supply an addict with minimal maintenance doses does, in some cases, constitute a medical need.

4. A physician is free to evolve his own methods of treatment without interference from Government or Police authorities.

5. There is no "state registration" of addicts but doctors are asked to inform the Home Office of any drug addicts coming under their care.

6. An addict is not committing any offence unless he is in possession of drugs unlawfully.

7. He is regarded as a sick person. Even if convicted of an offence under the Act, he may be put on probation provided he accepts medical treatment.

8. While under treatment voluntarily, the addict is not bound to follow his physician's advice.

9. The number of addicts known to the Home Office represents, for all practical purposes, the actual number of addicts in the country and there is no evidence of organised illicit traffic.

10. Drug addiction presents no real problem in the United Kingdom.

REFERENCES

1. Banks, A. Leslie: Social Aspects of Disease. Ed. Arnold & Co., 1953.
2. Bett, W. R.: William Halsted, cocaine pioneer and addict. Brit. J. Addiction 49: Nos. 1 & 2. Jan.–July, 1952.
3. Memorandum as to duties of doctors and dentists. Dangerous Drugs Act. 1920 to 1932. Home Office, Oct. 1948.
4. Report of Departmental Committee on Morphine and Heroin Addiction. Ministry of Health. H. M. Stationary Office, 1926.
5. The Traffic in Opium and Other Dangerous Drugs. Report to The U.N. by H. M. Government in the United Kingdom of Great Britain and Northern Ireland for 1954.
6. East, Sir Norwood: The British Government report to the U.N. on the traffic in opium and other drugs. Brit. J. Addiction 49: Nos. 1 & 2, Jan.–July, 1952.
7. Dent, J. Y.: Apomorphine in the treatment of addiction to "Other Drugs." Brit. J. Addiction 50: No. 1, April, 1953.
8. Dent, J. Y.: Anxiety and its Treatment, ed. 3. London, Skeffington, 1955.
9. Communication from the Community of St. Mary the Virgin, Spelthorne St. Mary, Thorpe, Surrey: The problem of the alcoholic. Brit. J. Addiction 49: Nos. 1 & 2, Jan.–July, 1952.
10. Spencer Paterson, A.: Addiction to morphia and allied drugs, some recent developments. Post-Grad. M. J. 30: No. 350, Dec. 1954.

X. Looking Forward

ON JANUARY 14, 1955, Senator Frederick G. Payne of Maine presented to the Senate a joint resolution "to provide for more effective control of narcotic drugs, and for other purposes." Co-sponsored by forty-two other Senators, it was sent to the Interdepartmental Committee, consisting of representatives from the Departments of State; Treasury; Defense; Health, Education and Welfare; and Justice. This Committee requested the Committee on Public Health of The New York Academy of Medicine to study the bill and submit a report.

By the time the Subcommittee on Drug Addiction of the Committee on Public Health had an opportunity to convene, it was informed that the narcotics bill had not come out of committee. However, the Subcommittee was requested to consider the narcotics problem and propose measures for suitable legislation.

This move, in itself a very healthy and progressive one, resulted in a report published in August, 1955,* which gives an excellent appraisal of the existing situation in the United States. The Subcommittee has covered the history of legislation to control drug addiction; our present laws; their effect on the addict and on the private physician; drug addiction and crime, methods of treatment, and other related subjects. It has drawn conclusions based on the effectiveness of existing laws and made proposals for future legislation. It considers the Payne Bill's commendable provisions to be overbalanced by its continued punitive approach and its severe penalties. But regardless of the eventual fate of this bill, it has served a useful purpose because it is actually responsible for this sound report.

---

*Report on Addiction. The New York Academy of Medicine. Committee on Public Health, Subcommittee on Drug Addiction. Bull. New York Acad. Med. *31*: 592-607, 1955.

The Academy's six point proposal is so carefully thought out and inclusive that I wish to quote it in its entirety. Designed to achieve the objective of stamping out drug addiction as completely as possible, it is concerned with stopping the formation of new addicts and rehabilitating as many present addicts as is possible. It also wisely includes a proposal for medical supervision of individuals already addicted to narcotic drugs who are resistant to rehabilitation.

Prefacing the proposals is the statement that in order to achieve its objectives, it will be necessary to institute all measures, not just one.

SIX POINT PROGRAM*

"1. There should be a change in attitude toward the addict. He is a sick person, not a criminal. That he may commit criminal acts to maintain his drug supply is recognized; but it is unjust to consider him criminal simply because he uses narcotic drugs.

"2. The Academy believes that the most effective way to eradicate drug addiction is to take the profit out of the illicit drug traffic. The causes of addiction are cited as: maladjustment; underprivilege; broken home; poverty. Such conditions may well be contributory factors, but they are not of themselves the prime cause. Rather, profit looms large as the principal factor.

"In seeking ways to reduce the formation of new addicts, it is helpful to consider the mechanisms of addiction and its spread. Availability of the drug, ignorance, curiosity and persuasion are the necessary ingredients for initiating drug use. Curiosity and the need to conform to the behavioral code of his age-group is probably a factor in attracting an adolescent to the use of narcotic drugs. In this group, it is common practice to designate a non-user as 'chicken' or as 'a square' if he refuses to use drugs. For certain individuals the ridicule of his fellows is unbearable; even though not wishing to do so, he finds himself taking drugs, and ultimately an addict.

"Prospective users are furnished drugs by the 'pusher' until

*Ibid., pp. 603-607. Quoted by permission of the Bulletin of The New York Academy of Medicine.

addiction occurs. But once this has taken place, the addict is required to pay for every dose and thus a life of slavery begins.
Therefore, the formation of new addicts is principally the result
of commercial exploitation. Contained in the preamble of the
Payne Bill is this assertion: 'Illicit traffic in narcotic drugs for
profit are the primary and sustaining sources of addiction . . .' [sic]
If all profit were removed from dealings in narcotic drugs, there
would be no incentive in giving away these drugs in an attempt to
addict others.

"The addict should be able to obtain his drug at low cost under
Federal control, in conjunction with efforts to have him undergo
withdrawal. Under this plan, these addicts, as sick persons, would
apply for medical care and supervision. Criminal acts would no
longer be necessary in order to obtain a supply of drugs and there
would be no incentive to create new addicts. Agents and black
markets would disappear from lack of patronage. Since about
eighty-five per cent of the 'pushers' on the streets are said to be
addicts, they would be glad to forego this dangerous occupation if
they were furnished with their needed drug. Thus the bulk of the
traffic would substantially disappear. By its very nature this traffic
requires many agents scattered in diffuse neighborhoods. If a few
unaddicted 'pushers' were all that remained to carry on the trade,
they would present a lesser problem for apprehension by the
police.

"3. An integral part of the program would be medical supervision of existing addicts, with vigorous efforts towards their rehabilitation. No particular philosophy of stamping out drug
addiction and traffic has an exclusive proprietary of rehabilitation. Whatever the method it must include a plan and operation
to rehabilitate the existing addict. This objective carries three
parts: 1) persuasion of the addict to undergo treatment and
rehabilitation; 2) appraisal of the methods of treatment and
their success; 3) supervision of addicts who are resistant to undergoing treatment or refractory to treatment.

"By a change in social attitude which would regard them as
sick persons, and by relieving them of the economic oppression of
attempting to obtain their supply of drug at an exorbitant price,
it will be possible to reach existing addicts in an orderly dignified

way, not as probationed persons, or sentenced criminals. They would come under supervision in the interest of health, not because of entanglement with the law. Thereafter, on a larger scale and in a humanitarian atmosphere, there would be opportunity to apply persuasion to undergo rehabilitation. It is reasonable to expect that more might accept the opportunity.

"It is a temptation to think of addicts as a homogeneous group, whereas all that they have in common is their addiction. They differ in age, personality, constitution, social and cultural environment, and length of time of addiction. Each addict is therefore an individual therapeutic problem. Present methods to convert addicts into abstainers have comprised removal of the drug and then institution of rehabilitative measures. Physical dependence on drugs can be removed by the withdrawal treatment. The mental and emotional fixations, however, are to be overcome only through the individual's own efforts and desires. Psychotherapy cannot be forced upon him with any hope of lasting benefit. Rehabilitation of severely addicted individuals to the point where they abstain from drugs for the remainder of their lives has been shown to be an extremely slow process with an equally slow rate of success. The present therapeutic regimen has suffered from premature termination of support to the patient. There is a need to maintain continuing contact with recovered addicts so that they may be helped in resisting the return to use of a drug in stress situations. A counseling service for them is urgently needed.

"Not all the addicts subscribing to the proposed plan will agree at once to undergo treatment. In accord with this concept that treatment of the addict must be individualistic, the Academy believes that in appropriate institutions it might be well to try a reverse order. After the addict has undergone education and rehabilitation and has obtained employment, there might be more success in inducing him to give up the drug. It has been asserted that many addicted individuals become enslaved between the ages of seventeen and twenty. It is evident that addiction then occurs before the individual has had an opportunity to acquire a skill by which he can earn an honest living. If he is furnished his drug in required amount, he may be willing to be trained in a useful trade. When he has been enabled to maintain his livelihood with his former fears and strains removed, he may be willing to give up drugs. Thus a change in social attitude and a different therapeutic approach in appropriate instances might offer more success in persuading an addict to undergo treatment and in the results of that treatment.

"Addicts resistant to undertaking therapy and continuously refractory to therapy, despite all efforts, should be supplied legally and cheaply with the minimum amount of their drug needs; and efforts to persuade them to undergo rehabilitation should be continued.

"It is suggested therefore that there be developed a program whereby sufficient amounts of drugs can be legally and inexpensively supplied to addicts, while attempts are being made to have them undergo treatment. This service for narcotic addicts should be instituted in dispensary-clinics, preferably attached to hospitals, whether Federal, municipal or voluntary. No person should be given drugs at such a service clinic unless he is willing to enter a hospital for evaluation of his drug needs. After careful medical evaluation he should receive at cost from the service clinic the amount of drug which it has been medically determined that he requires.

"The service clinic should be in operation twenty-four hours a day, seven days a week, to insure that no addict has the excuse that he could not obtain his supply from a legitimate source and was thus forced by his discomfort to seek his supply from illicit dispensers. At no time should he be given a supply of narcotics adequate for more than two days; if he is found to have sold or given away any of the supply to another person, he shall be liable to commitment to a hospital with attempted rehabilitation.

"If an addict uses more than the amount of drug supplied to him for the prescribed period, he should not be penalized so long as he returns to the service clinic for his legitimate supply. But in the event of such a lapse from the pattern of his consumption of drugs, he should be re-admitted to the hospital for another evaluation of his drug needs.

"Needless to say, all addicts receiving drugs from the service clinic or entering a hospital for evaluation and treatment should be photographed and fingerprinted; copies of such photographs and fingerprints should be sent to a central agency, while one copy is retained at the original clinic. By means of a punchcard system monthly checks should be made by the central agency to insure that an addict is not obtaining supplies from more than one clinic. If such a violation is found to exist, the offending addict shall immediately be subject to commitment as a hospital patient.

"It is visualized that such service clinics will be established all over the country. Thus it will be possible for an addict desiring to change his residence to transfer from one service clinic to another without encountering difficulties in maintaining his supply. Whenever an addict wishes to go to another community, he will notify his regular clinic of his intent. The clinic will in turn notify the central agency of his new location and will forward to the new clinic the record of his evaluation and his conduct at the original clinic.

"Strictly enforced, these safeguards should eliminate any possibility of the use of the illicit market and should insure that only those with intractable addiction are actually receiving narcotics. It is also postulated that there will be no laxity in enforcing provisions for failure to abide by the service clinic regulations.

"Much space, perhaps a disproportionate amount, has been devoted to detailing the provisions for furnishing drugs to the addicts who refuse treatment. Actually it is hoped that this group will be small in number and constantly diminishing. For, all the while, unrelenting attempts would be made to persuade the resistant addict to undergo therapy to break the habit.

"It will be seen that this recommendation is a humane, reasonable, and promisingly effective method of distribution. It should be remembered that every addict will get his drug. Under the present laws to do that he must 'push,' rob, steal, burglarize or commit forgery. For, he is desperate when he is without drugs.

"This part of the program containing provision for distribution of drugs to addicts has been opposed on the basis of previous short-lived experience with drug clinics. Admittedly some of the clinics were abused; others had success. In any event, there was insufficient time for them to demonstrate their merits. There is an aura of mystery surrounding the preemptory and premature closing of them. From all available facts it would appear that they were closed, not because they had failed, but because operation of them did not accord with the prevailing philosophy of a punitive approach to a criminal problem.

"4. It is proposed that there be no relaxation in the efforts toward complete and permanent elimination of the supply of illegal narcotic drugs and that provisions for suppression of illegal traffic be retained. It is the Academy's belief that the suggested plan to remove the profit would diminish illicit traffic. Whatever illicit operations were left after its application should be vigorously eradicated by appropriate laws, their enforcement, and provision for suitable penalties. Here illicit traffic should be re-defined to allow provision of drugs to addicts under medical supervision and treatment. This procedure should be surrounded by suitable safeguards. If anyone receiving drugs under the supportive plan should be found attempting to receive or to be receiving supplies from more than one clinic or from an illicit market, or if he be found attempting to sell or actually selling any of his supply to another person, he should be liable to commitment to a hospital with attempted rehabilitation. Thus he should be controlled as a sick person, not as a criminal.

"Initially, it would be essential to provide the trained staff necessary to apprehend the peddlers, wholesalers and importers. It goes without saying that this group will not give up its lucrative business without a struggle. But a dearth of drug users, combined with severe penalties for dealing in narcotics, could be expected to put an end to the illicit drug traffic within a relatively short time.

"It should be emphasized that the law should draw a distinction between the addict and non-addict in its provision. The convicted non-addict trafficker should feel its full force.

"5. Adolescent addicts are reported to have said that they would not have taken drugs in the first place if they had known that they were going to become addicted. Such statements of youth are a strong argument for a good educational program for young people. The adult user, too, reports that he did not know the dangers of narcotic drugs when he began their use. If such reports are correct, it would appear that an educational program for adults as well as for adolescents is needed.

"Combined with the medical care of narcotic addicts and severe penalties for trafficking in drugs, there should be an adequate program of education for adults, teachers and youth. By means of all education media, including radio, television, the public press, forum, lecture, books and pamphlets, there should be a concerted effort at informing the public of the dangers of narcotic drugs. Furthermore, there should be impressed upon the population the need to treat addicts, to apprehend illicit drug dealers, and to avoid the use of such drugs except under medical supervision.

"6. One of the great difficulties in planning for a medical approach in the care and supervision of addicts is the lack of accurate information on their number. So long as they are stamped as criminals that difficulty will exist. It is a merit of the medical approach that by adopting the proper attitude toward them, it should be possible to study the epidemiology of drug addiction and acquire information about the magnitude and pathogenesis of the disease.

"By means of the records accumulated at the central agency, it would be possible to have at all times an accurate count of the known resistant addicts in the country. It would also be possible to know how many addicts were undergoing treatment for their illness and how many relapsed after a period of abstinence. Data on the length of abstinence from narcotic drugs and therefore on the success of various types of treatment would be obtainable. On the basis of such information, research could be focused more readily on the 'why' of addiction and on improved methods of treatment. There seems little possibility of learning the 'why' of addiction until narcotic addicts can be studied under conditions more nearly approximating normal existence than do those of a hospital, excellent though it may be.

"So much has been stated about the relation of drug addiction and crime, particularly about the need for drugs leading to crime, that the Academy is moved to state that realistically it has no extravagant expectations that the proposed plan will completely eliminate crime. If a person was a criminal before he became a drug addict, it is not necessarily to be expected that he will cease to follow his predilections for crime just because he no longer is an addict. Perhaps it is fair to state that crime arising from the need for drugs may diminish; but criminal acts committed for other reasons may not decrease.

"It is the opinion of the Academy that this program, taken in its entirety, is a reasonable and humane approach to the solution of drug addiction. It must be frankly admitted that there is no ideal or perfect solution. Of the two possible approaches to the solution of the problem, the punitive as against the medical, it becomes a matter of judgment as to which gives the more promise of effectiveness and contains fewer points of vulnerability. In judging between them the Academy believes that the evidence is preponderantly in favor of its proposed program as the more promising means of ridding the nation of drug addiction."

*   *   *

The report of the Academy opens new vistas for therapeutic experimentation. It suggests the exploration of forms of therapy removed from the aura of the correctional institution. By affirming addiction as a medical illness their recommendation may produce a decisive historical change and encourage the physician to help solve this major medical and social problem as he has others.

There has been and will be a vast amount of pressure against such a program, on the grounds that once a person is addicted to drugs he becomes a criminal personality, unamenable to treatment. There is a growing feeling, however, that the country has much to gain, and—in the light of a growing problem—little to lose, by a new approach emphasizing constructive scientific thinking.

APPENDIX
An Addict's Glossary

A few of the commoner terms in the addict vocabulary are given below. While by no means complete, the list does offer one common ground for the physician meeting his addict patient, and his familiarity with such terms may reassure the patient and indicate a willingness to understand his problems. This special language not only is most extensive but varies with both the times and the locale. It is interesting to speculate on the possible psychological derivation of some of these words. For example, a drug peddler is frequently referred to as "mother."

BANG (DRIVE, CHARGE, JOLT, KICK). The excitement felt immediately after injecting into a vein.

BELLY HABIT. This refers to a habit maintained by taking the drug orally. It most frequently refers to opium.

BENNY (PEP PILLS, JOLLY BEANS). Benzedrine.

BLACK STUFF (TAR, GUM). Crude opium.

BREAK THE HABIT (KICK IT). To get off drugs.

CAP. Capsules containing heroin. Addicts refer to their habits in terms of both how much they pay and how many "caps" they take a day.

C (COKE). Cocaine.

CHIPPING (A CHIPPY HABIT, JOY POPPING, PLAY AROUND). Using drugs occasionally without being addicted.

CHUCK HABIT. This refers to the excessive craving for food, especially starches, which occurs following withdrawal.

COASTING (ON THE NOD). This describes the period between shots of drugs during which a patient is pleasantly drowsy, unaware of time elapsing.

COLD TURKEY. An abrupt withdrawal of drugs. It refers to the "goose flesh" which occurs during withdrawal.

CONNECTION (DEALER, MOTHER). Either a person who knows a source of drugs or one who actually supplies them.

COOL (SMOOTH, REAL GONE). A complimentary term referring to someone who is poised, unruffled.

CROAKER. A physician.

CUT. Adulterating drugs, usually with sugar.

FUN (TOY). 5.8 grains of opium. Opium is sold by the "fun."

GOOF BALL (YELLOW JACKET). Sleeping pill.

GRAPEVINE. The addict world, in or out of prison.

HARRY (H, HORSE, JUNK, WHITE STUFF). Heroin.

JUNK (MOJO, STUFF, GOODS). Any kind of narcotic.

JUNKIE. A drug addict.

MAIN LINE. A vein.

POT (MUGGLES, TEA, WEED). Marijuana.

REEFER. Marijuana cigarette.

SCRIP. A physician's prescription.

SNOW. Cocaine powder.

SPEEDBALL. Combination of cocaine with heroin or other opiates.

TURN ON. To give a non-addict his first shot, an act which most addicts are reluctant to perform.

YEN. An intense craving for narcotics, even if the addict is not at the time on drugs.

INDEX

Rehabilitation, 129-147 (*see also*
  Treatment)
  aim of, 138, 164 *ff*
  ambulatory hospitalization in, 139-
    141
  cancelled appointments in, 135-136
  community groups in, 143-144
  conditions favoring, 99-100
  diagnosis of needs in, 134-135
  duration of, 129
  environment in, 146-147
  Narcotics Anonymous in, 144-146
  physician's role in, 129, 130-133
  psychiatric care in, 141-143
  psychiatrist's role in, 129
  relapses in, 136-139
  success of, 129
Relapse, 54-55, 94-95, 129
  duration of, 97
  morphine, 139
  pharmacologic factor in, 54
  physician's role in, 136
  withdrawal symptoms in, 54
Respiration, and morphine, 51
Rorschach, of addict, 60-62

Secobarbital, 125
Self
  attitudes toward, of addict, 69-75
  -esteem, of addict, 72, 79
  -image, idealized, of addict, 73-74
  -preoccupation and self-destruction,
    69-70
Sensorium, of addict, 60
Sex drive
  and addiction, 64-65, 69
  and marijuana, 30
  and morphine, 45-46, 48
  and opium, 18
Shock, and morphine, 47
Social pathology, 83-100
Soneryl, 154
Stimulants, dangerous, 27-33
Suggestion, and morphine, 49
Sulfadiazine, 50

Symptomatology, 104
Symptom (s)
  addiction as, 57
  hysterical conversion, 122
  simulated, 118
  withdrawal
    in animals, 45
    "artificial," 51
    barbiturate, 126
    basis of, 52
    and hypoglycemia, 119
    manifestations of, 122
    and Nalline, 51, 110
    in newborn, 20
    in relapse, 54
    treatment of, 121-124
    and morphine, 2, 116-117

Thebaine, 24
Tolerance, drug, 26, 42, 50-52
Treatment (*see also* Rehabilitation)
  ambulatory hospital, 73
  for barbiturate addiction, 126
  clinic, in U. S., 1-13
  of cocaine poisoning, 29
  compulsory, 5
  dilemma of, 111-112
  duration of, 97-99
  in England, 148, 153-157
  final stage of, 147
  following relapse, 126
  hospital
    for barbiturate withdrawal, 35
    termination of, 126-127
  Nalline in, 26 (*see also* Nalline)
  number of
    and duration of addiction, 97
    in female addicts, 97
    in law violators, 97
    in physicians, 98
  of opiate poisoning, 26
  out-patient, 73
  and rehabilitation, 129-147
  of relapse, 136-139
  psychiatric, 35, 73
  voluntary, 99-100